FORBIDDEN ROOTS

www.mascotbooks.com

Forbidden Roots: A Memoir of Late-Discovery Adoption

For more information, please contact
Mascot Books, an imprint of Amplify Publishing Group:
620 Herndon Parkway, Suite 320
Herndon, VA 20170
info@mascotbooks.com

Library of Congress Control Number: 2021925890

CPSIA Code: PRV0322A
ISBN-13: 978-1-63755-187-5

Printed in the United States

TO ALL THOSE INVOLVED IN
THE ADOPTION TRIANGLE.

FORBIDDEN ROOTS

A MEMOIR
OF LATE-DISCOVERY ADOPTION

FRED NICORA

CONTENTS

1 | PREFACE: PEACE

PART I: NEW REALITIES

5 | CHAPTER 1: THE DISCOVERY (OCTOBER 2000)

The Search Begins—9

Her Partner—15

A New Normality—18

Back to the Search—23

35 | CHAPTER 2: THE SEARCH MUST GO ON (NOVEMBER 2000)

He's Down Under—44

A Visit to Maureen—45

About the Brookshiers—49

The Bastard before You—53

Getting the Brass Ring (DECEMBER 2000)—56

A Comfortable Diversion—58

Look, Ma. I'm Famous. (FEBRUARY 2001)—61

More about the Brookshiers—62

63 | CHAPTER 3: MEETING THE RELATIVES

Don's Aunt Ina (MARCH 2001)—63

Adjustments and Aftershocks—66

Brother Tim (JULY 2001)—74

Brothers John and Guy—Toledo (AUGUST 2001)—75

83 | CHAPTER 4: MILE MARKERS

A Dreadful Tangent (SEPTEMBER 2001)—83

My First Anniversary—Alone (OCTOBER 2001)—85

In Search of Ron and Edna—the Long Haul—88

PART II: NEW CRISES, NEW LIVES, NEW ROUTINES

97 | CHAPTER 5: GRACE'S CRISIS (MARCH 2003)

105 | CHAPTER 6: A LITTLE TOO LITTLE, A LITTLE TOO LATE (APRIL 2003)

Life in the Balance (May 2003)—111

A Little Help from Some Friends—119

Trying New Identities—123

Life on the Road (August 2003)—132

Shifting into Final Gear—135

139 | CHAPTER 7: TIME TO MOVE ON (JANUARY 2004)

Tish the Dish—145

Putting an End to It—148

Guy and the Avengers—150

Settling into New Digs—155

159 | CHAPTER 8: THE WINDS OF CHANGE (AUGUST 2004)

PART III: NEW INSIGHTS FROM THE PAST

165 | CHAPTER 9: RECONNECTING (MAY 2005)

Out of Nowhere (May 2005)—167

More than Answers—169

Summer's Loose Ends—173

179 | CHAPTER 10: A SIDE TRIP INTO THE PAST (JUNE 2006)

PART IV: PUTTING THE PIECES TOGETHER

189 | CHAPTER 11: LINCOLN, VICKSBURG, AND RON (AUGUST 2006)

201 | CHAPTER 12: IT'S TIME TO BURY THE PAST (NOVEMBER 2006)

207 | EPILOGUE

209 | ACKNOWLEDGMENTS

211 | ABOUT THE AUTHOR

PREFACE

PEACE

November 2006

M oonlight dominated the barren landscape. November in Wisconsin was decorated with only skeletons of what was once a lush forestland. A parched streambed longed for its thirst to be quenched by the April storms. Gone were the multitudes of biological genius. All living things waited desperately for the vibrancy of spring. The seasons of the upper Midwest brought a contrast, a reshaping of what used to be familiar territory. No longer were the summer trails visible. Deer foraged new paths. The raccoons, possums, fox, and squirrels sought hibernation as a refuge from the cold, harsh reality of winter. Many creatures couldn't bear its biting reality and had left. Now, created by the death of autumn leaves, a new, unfamiliar landscape emerged. Eventually, the leaves integrated their once-vibrant living souls into the morbid recirculation of life as the

I

plants, insects, birds, and other forms of higher life consumed the simplistic forms of life.

I knew this had to happen. Whether it was the end or simply a new beginning, I hadn't a clue. I had been here before. But this time was different. This time I had control; I would make the choices. Logic would say there was no way this could have had so much control over my life, but it was all consuming. For years I had tried to bury it, tried to eradicate it, and tried to forget about it, but I couldn't. I tried. At last I felt peace. Or maybe it was just the start of a new trail.

Standing on top of the wooded ravine, I could see the shadows of all those who had been here before me. Some were perhaps twenty, some fifty, and even the eldest were over one hundred years old. The ash, poplar, maple, and oak were the witnesses. They had seen many here, and perhaps they had observed a few burials. The last shovel of earth had been laid, and I was done with my work. After six years it was early November in the comfort of a remote corner of vast woodlands. Millions of years have carved the peaceful valley that unfolded before me, gently winding its way on to the eternal shores of Lake Michigan. Yet it was only the last six years that have brought me to where I am—made me what I am today. I longed for an ending so peaceful, so serene. I had done my best. I always did. I missed you.

It was a clear evening with a sparse smattering of clouds, similar to that fateful night in 2000. Although I was born in 1959, I have lived two lives since then. The first was one full of optimism and significance; the second started in 2000. I have no clue why it happened. I didn't ask to be here, but once again it was fate, the meaning of which I had grown to hate and grown to love. Like a lethal addiction, it grabbed me and reshaped me. It tantalized me and repulsed me. It has also given me everything, and at the same time it has taken everything I thought was me. In silence, I took a moment to reflect.

PART I

NEW REALITIES

CHAPTER 1

THE DISCOVERY

OCTOBER 2000

Attending my twin uncles' sixtieth birthday party on a Saturday night in late October 2000, I was glad to see my relatives. Growing up, Rich and Bob had always been around, and I always looked up to them. We had recently moved back to southeastern Wisconsin to be closer to extended family. Our three children had lived their entire lives in Minnesota, only to see my relatives when an occasional holiday trip offered a brief visit. My parents had died—my father in 1993 and my mother in 1997. Both died of cancer. It was awful. I had been able to make many weekly trips through the final year of each of their lives, and eventually I observed them complete their morphed journey to a place unknown to the living. As our children were young, it made the reality of bringing the entire family down for the six-hour drive impractical. While my wife and

I enjoyed living in the Twin Cities of Minneapolis-Saint Paul, we missed the ability to share holidays with family and have our children learn what growing up with family meant.

Shortly after arriving at the restaurant, we found a place to sit at one of the large rectangular banquet tables that ran nearly the length of the hall. Many familiar faces were at the table already seated. My mother's side of my family was large and very connected. Everyone I remember growing up with from her side was there. It felt good to be back home. My uncle Bob, one of the guests of honor, had also invited my cousin Fredlyn from my father's side of the family. She was the only witness to this event from my father's side. Technically, she was a cousin in that she was my dad's sister's daughter. Since my parents had me later in life, however, she was old enough to have a daughter my same age. As a matter of fact, her daughter and I graduated in the same high school class. Deb, her daughter, knew me inside and out. Not only were we cousins but we were also friends. That was one of the missed clues. Families of three, in the late 1950s and 1960s, with older parents were often different kinds of families. Many more clues were still waiting to be uncovered.

After getting everyone settled, I proceeded to get us all something to drink. Although there was an open beer and wine bar, something told me it was a Scotch and water night. Had I known what lay ahead, I surely would have made it a double. When I returned to the table, my wife, Sylvia, had a curious look on her face. I asked her if everything was all right. She turned and pointed to my great-aunt Lydia.

"Is that Alice?" she asked.

"No," I replied. "That's Lydia."

While the question was certainly justifiable, as Sylvia hadn't interacted much with that side of the family, I knew there was a deeper meaning. Alice was known to get things confused. But Lydia, on the contrary, was known to be sharp as a tack, even though she had to be well into her eighties.

"Why?" I probed.

"Well, she just said she's known you since the day you were adopted," she replied.

"Adopted? What do you mean?"

"She said, 'I've known Freddy since the day he was adopted.'"

I fractured. I went to find Lydia. As I approached, she greeted me.

"Hi, Freddy, I was just talking to your lovely wife. Oh, your children are beautiful."

"Hi. Did you tell Sylvia you've known me since the day I was adopted?"

Her smile disintegrated, and her skin paled. Her eyes shifted back and forth as her hands rose and framed her face like two bookends.

"Oh my God, you didn't know?"

"What do you mean?"

"Didn't they tell you? I'm so sorry. I shouldn't have—"

I heard the conversation fading. Time stood still. It all made sense, yet nothing made sense. Who knew? They all knew. It was as if someone had stuck the two blades of an eggbeater in my head, one in each ear, and turned it on high. The past, present, and future blended together into a murky abyss. Suddenly my life had no boundary, no structure. I felt naked. I couldn't stay. I had to get out. Quickly, I gathered my family—the only family I was certain of—and left. As word spread throughout the gathering, the alarms sounded. I saw several of them emerge from the door as we pulled out of the parking lot. "Them"—the thought seemed foreign. I never thought of my family in terms of "them." I always thought we were a "we." The fable "The Emperor's New Clothes" took on a whole new meaning.

The rest of the night and the following day were a blur, an endless hunt of which the main purpose was to capture the truth. I felt my only hope was to surprise those with knowledge and capture the fragments of truth before the tracks could be covered. Door after door led to little additional knowledge, only an affirmation that yes, indeed, I was adopted, and I was the only one who didn't know. One of the small pieces of knowledge I obtained was from my father's sister. She told me my dad said she thought my biological father was a professor. She also confided that it was my dad, her brother, who was the one who insisted on my ignorance. His family had grown up during the Depression. His parents were the first among a growing population to seek divorce to solve their problems. Unfortunately, it was the children who suffered. My father, three years of age at the time, spent time in the county home. He was determined not to have me experience the horrors of being an orphan. Suddenly my identity was reshaped. I was the family's skeleton. I was the dirty little secret no one wanted to talk about. I was the one who could silence a room.

On Sunday night I needed to process what had happened. I started to turn inward. We lived by the shores of Lake Michigan, an endless path of "barking" sand. The sand is known for its fine, granulated consistency that when walked upon would bark. That night not only would it bark but it also would engage in an infinite dialogue of analytical self-reflective babble. My two companions were my dogs. One was a rottweiler and blue heeler mix named Ajax. Since the day we adopted him, his intellectual stubbornness created an endless struggle for the alpha position in our household. Despite his destructive tendencies, I could not bring myself to abandon him. The other was a handsome golden lab. Ever yielding to his masters, Luke was the envy of every other dog owner. His gentle manner was a comfort to my children and a guardian to Sylvia. He appeared to us one hot late-summer day with his mother by his side. His tags led us to his owner, who explained he was the last of a litter and offered him to us, as we seemed to be a good fit. As we walked, the two made a perfect polar match to the opposite realities of my newfound life.

The minutes turned into hours, and the footsteps turned into miles. I lost myself. Endless waves of raw emotion ripped and reformulated my soul. Inside I found my parents alive again. I buried and grieved for them years ago. That night our relationships had been resurrected. *Why? Why hadn't you told me? Why hadn't I discovered this fact? Why did I discover it?* A sparsely clouded moonlit night drew me further and further along my journey, orchestrated by the relentless sounds of the pounding waves. Each wave challenged who I was, what I believed, and what I trusted to be reality. Every relationship was challenged, regurgitated, and redigested. As the intensity of the emotional gale grew, the riptides of revelations reduced me to a sobbing amorphous blob huddled in the sand. Only the occasional comfort of my companions reshaped me into something recognizable—something to pull together, to wander on farther. As the night grew deeper, the northern lights began to display their glory. Spirits of a distant unknown land performed their glory ahead. Who were they? What did they want? An earlier rain had left pools of water captured by depressions in the sand. Misted sculptures began to emerge and join the gala in the sky. The barking sand below my feet ordered me to press on. Every question, every thought, that poured into my head filled the ever-increasing void with chaos. Yet I was alive, perhaps for the first time in my life.

As the eastern horizon began to glow in anticipation of the upcoming sunrise, I found myself wondering how far north I had walked. It was Monday. It must be around three, maybe three thirty in the morning. I had to be at work by eight. I needed to turn around; I needed to find my way home. About an hour on my return, I recognized the beach ahead. It was Amsterdam Beach. I was six miles from home. My return home was as timeless as my journey out. My mind and emotions raced at deafening speed. As sunlight gradually erased the darkness, other walkers appeared on the beach. I periodically darted into the edge of the woods, which defined the edge of the enlightened sand and the emptiness of the darkened forest. I couldn't be seen. Yes, I was the emperor, and I was acutely aware I was naked and exposed. I didn't understand that to them I was fully clothed. When I returned home, it was already six thirty. Many nighttime beach walks would follow; however, the encroaching change of seasons would soon halt my ability to walk along the beach. The following spring they resumed.

THE SEARCH BEGINS

I couldn't wait for Monday morning to arrive. I knew the only way to cement my belief in my newfound reality was to have the state, my trusted government, confirm my nightmare or expose the sickness of the hoax. As a high school teacher, I had the first period of the day as my preparation period. I could call the Milwaukee courthouse Monday morning to end this charade. Certainly they couldn't, and they wouldn't, hold the truth from me. It was my life. It was my truth. But I soon found out they didn't hold the answer. It would be another phone call away. Adoption information was contained in an obscure government building in the state capital, Madison. *At last*, I thought, *I would soon find the many answers to my questions*. First, am I really adopted, or was this just some odd misunderstanding? Second, if I was adopted, where was I born? Who were my parents? Do I have brothers and sisters? And finally, the mother of all questions: Who am I? The odd thing was, I didn't want new parents. I loved my parents. They provided a good life for me. I buried my parents. But I wanted something on which to stand. Ever since Sylvia told me what Lydia said, it felt like there was nothing below me. I don't mean that figuratively, but literally. While I could see the floor beneath my feet, it felt like there was nothing down there. It was like an endless free fall. While I wasn't afraid of the feeling itself, I knew I wanted it to end.

Finally, I made my contact. At last the person on the other end of the line held the key to unlock my identity. After taking my information and a brief period on hold, the answer came. It was true. This was no sick hoax. The only misunderstanding was mine. While it was true the state could answer my first question, the following questions were more complex. Even though it was my life and my truth, I had no right, no legal access to my reality. The voice on the other end of the phone was allowed to know everything about me. She was reading it, purposefully leaving out any relevant detail that would provide the slightest clue about who I was or where I came from. But if I paid money, filled out the right forms, and waited six to eight weeks, I could get a copy of the nonidentification information. This would give me background information about the circumstances surrounding my adoption, but any information that could lead to my birth parents' identities would be redacted. Only after I reviewed the nonidentification information could I pursue finding out about my biological past and my genetic heritage. This, too, I found out followed a less than direct path. I could write a letter to my biological mother describing who I was and why I wanted to find out who I was; however, it came with a risk. If she, for whatever reason, decided not to let me know, I would have to wait five years before I could try again. If at that time she again decided not to reveal her identity, I would lose my chance for life. The path was terminal. Once I completed the letter, I was to send it to the voice on the phone, who would read it, via phone, to my biological mother. Finally, should she agree to release my identity, only then could I obtain a copy of my original birth certificate. All these years I had been running around with the imposter, the fake birth certificate, which fraudulently claimed to be the "original." In the adoption circuit, this was the coveted brass ring. I agreed. "Send me the forms."

As the days passed, I found my impatience and hunger growing. My feet refused to find solid ground, and I was becoming accustomed to the feeling of the never-ending free fall. Every other aspect of my life became irrelevant. I could hear my children speak, but it wasn't me who was answering them. I saw myself complete the ritualistic tasks of life, but felt detached from my body as I observed the mechanical movements of my job, housework, and their associated duties. Sylvia became crystallized. Her beauty was apparent, but she seemed frozen and distant. I knew I was teaching, but I relied on safe, noncommunicative forms of instruction. "Read chapter five, complete the following worksheet, work on your projects." The blinding light of my reality had kidnapped my ability to direct my thought and formulate reason. I was obsessed. Even though the brilliant intensity of my new reality was burning the eyes from my head, I couldn't look away. Everything in my life seemed unfamiliar. It was no longer my life.

Surely the voice on the phone must understand I had been sentenced to limbo without a trial. Just give me a clue—something solid to hold on to. I was desperate. I called and called again. *Please give me some concrete piece of information to bring me back to solid ground.*

The response was kind yet stern. "We have laws to follow. Your forms should be there any day. Once we get the necessary forms and fees, we can start the process."

I started to feel like a second-class citizen. Before I found out I was allowed full access to all my own records, but now that I was adopted the same rules didn't apply. My rules were different. I played the game. I paid my taxes. But suddenly I became one of "them."

After many calls filled with futility, she agreed to give me more. "Your mother was twenty-two when you were born, and you were born in Cambridge, Wisconsin. No, wait, I'm sorry. It's Milwaukee. I have to go." Click.

What was that all about? It seemed as if she was just starting to move, and then she hung up. Maybe she has a conscience. Maybe she does care. I tried again.

"I've told you all I can. I have work to do." Click.

Why did she say Cambridge? I was familiar with Cambridge. I dated a girl from Cambridge when I went to UW–Stout. Cambridge was a small Wisconsin town somewhere in the middle of a triangle formed by Milwaukee, Chicago, and Rockford, Illinois. I recalled that Cambridge was where Rhoda was from. A banker's daughter, she was a passionate, energetic soul who seemed to enjoy life far beyond my abilities. Cambridge must have something to do with it. Somehow it comforted me to know my biological mother was from Rhoda's hometown. I reexamined my birth certificate and discovered county of birth wasn't far from mother's residence.

Cambridge also brought me back to my mother's family and her aunt Maggy. Maggy was one of Alice and Lydia's sisters, and she lived in Cambridge for a while. It was next to their brothers' business, a trucking company, where she eventually took root. My mother's stepmother was from a farm family in the Cambridge area. It also brought to mind another clue I had missed. In the early 1980s, my mother's family had a genealogy study completed. They were a proud people who valued their Polish-German heritage. In the mid-1980s, at a family gathering I attended, a discussion concerning the genealogy study became front and center. When I expressed my interest, my amazing ability to silence a room seemed to kick into high gear. Suddenly the prized piece of work seemed to be lost. No one remembered having a copy. But I was assured that once it could be tracked down, I could see it. I was living in California at the time, so the timeliness of finding the document was impossible during my short stay. Unfortunately, my interest endured. During a subsequent visit, I pressed my mother for a copy of the study I had been promised. She promptly delivered my request. Many years later, following my discovery, I noticed my entry was modified. I questioned whether it had been added after I asked to see it and recopied.

The forms arrived. They didn't seem to be anything special, so I wasn't sure why they were so important. But I filled them out as requested by the voice. The necessary fees were paid, and off they went to Madison. But my impatience grew. The state had fumbled the ball. The answers to the puzzle must be right in front of my face. I already knew my biological father was a professor. My mother must be from Cambridge. Among the other fragments of my biological mother's life I had been allowed to know was her age at the time of my birth. My next opportunity was an extended weekend Sylvia and I had off together. I packed up the family in the van, and we headed off on our adventure. Once in Cambridge, I went to the high school to see if anyone from the 1956 or 1957 class had similar features to my kids or me. Given my circumstances, the staff in the high school were more than happy to meet my requests to examine old yearbooks. They didn't seem to be aware of the fact adoptees weren't allowed to discover their identity. It was a success. Several girls had potential. One girl's eyes looked similar to my eldest daughter, Grace; another had my son's, Tony's, eyes. The third candidate seemed to combine many familial features. Now all I had to do was tie them to a four-year university and be unmarried at the time of my birth. My next stop was to the Cambridge Public Library. Buried within the vast collection of local history, I hoped there would be another clue. News of a reunion, a marriage announcement, perhaps even the documentation of a scandalous pregnancy, all could provide promise for choosing my next path. An unbelievable stroke of luck occurred. While describing my plight to the librarian, an elderly man approached. He introduced himself as the local historian for the Cambridge Historical Society. As I talked to him, he became quite sympathetic. "Meet me at the historical society in an hour," he suggested. "I think I can help you out."

My interim stop would be McDonald's. There I could regroup with my family. We could eat lunch, and I could digest my morning's feast. Sylvia saw great potential between candidates one and three. She eventually settled on one—the girl who looked similar to Grace. I still thought the third had the greatest promise.

When I arrived at the abandoned church, now housing the Cambridge Historical Society, he greeted me at the door. He promptly combed through the archives to isolate the reunion records of the girls I held in question. Given she must have attended a four-year university, we were able to narrow my options to one: Mary Miller. Of the candidates, she was the only one who went to a university and was not married at the time of my birth. Beyond that criteria, there was something else about Mary. She was my third candidate, and it was her smile. Madeline, my second daughter, can light up a room with her infectious smile. Mary seemed to radiate that same quality in her pictures. Three weeks had passed since I last felt solid ground below my feet. At last it returned. I had learned to function in my free-fall state; however, that didn't mean I had enjoyed or even accepted it. But at last the identification of a link to my forbidden past allowed me to have something to hold on to.

Later that week I received a call from the voice. They were expediting my record search. It seemed my persistent chain of phone calls touched a nerve. Their rationale was my late-discovery status. They reasoned that while the typical adoptee had grown up with the knowledge of their birth status my situation could allow for a slight deviation of protocol. Movement was finally underway. This had been a very good week. As the conversation continued, a problem surfaced. It seemed the adoption agency through which I was placed no longer existed. My records were lost. The voice agreed to contact me when they could be located. She assured me this happened periodically, and it should be a delay, not an end. In the late 1950s and 1960s, during the heyday of adoption placements, the demand for adoption services was high, and adoption service agencies flourished. But as options for avoiding and terminating unwanted pregnancies grew, the supply of available orphans diminished, as did the number of agencies. Records were consolidated and shuffled, but rarely lost. I didn't want to reveal my own detective work, as I feared it fell out of the state's expectations of acceptable behavior. The knowledge of my birth mother's face comforted me. It gave me patience as my case floated through the web of bureaucratic entanglement. But in the meantime, I would continue my own investigation.

HER PARTNER

My hunt for Mary came to a stall. Whereas I was able to find out her married name through the work of the volunteer at the Cambridge Historical Society, the trail quickly evaporated. Despite many attempts, I was unable to locate her. I turned down a new road. After high school Mary attended Lawrence University in Appleton, Wisconsin. A small private liberal arts college, Lawrence was located on the banks of the Fox River, about forty miles east of my home. It was known for its excellent prep programs, which often turned out to be the starting point for many prominent lawyers, doctors, and other professionals. I planned a trip to Lawrence the following weekend. Preliminary phone calls identified the hours the library was open, a place I hoped would further my journey and potentially reveal clues about Mary's partner.

On Sunday I arrived in Appleton. Although I had been to Appleton several times before, its streets were unfamiliar. A stop at a gas station provided me the map that would lead to the university, and hopefully the answers to my questions. As I proceeded to the campus, the atmosphere turned from that of an older Wisconsin rust belt town to one of a cloistered haven of youth and intellect. A combination of dignified brick-and-stone buildings contrasted with the newer concrete, steel, and glass structures of the modern movement. It was eight in the morning when I arrived. The library opened at nine. The campus mall was void of life, common in college towns following a Saturday night of personal explorations of the human experience. The cold and blustery November day exhibited crispness in the air, familiar to sun-filled Wisconsin winter days. It was a perfect time to explore. Walking by the houses and apartments gathered around the campus, exhibiting the signs of student life, I couldn't help but notice an occasional window and wonder, *Does that room have significance to me? Maybe Mary lived there. Could that be the secret apartment of a professor living a double life?*

Nine o'clock came and went. Once again I had slipped into an internal trance. Lost in a make-believe world of a forbidden childhood that could have been, I couldn't retrace the paths I took. When I checked my watch, it was already nine thirty, and I was far from the library. During that brief hour and a half, I managed to explore and live many potential lives. It was ten when I arrived at the library. Fearing an expulsion from the campus for tarnishing its brilliant, protected reputation, I simply explained I was working on a family genealogy study. Although I knew I could accept the shameful reality of my origin, I suspected others would be less tolerant of this bastard's intrusion. I had known several other adoptees prior to my discovery and always perceived myself to view them without prejudice. Why, then, had the revelation of my birth status affected me in such a way?

Examination of past annuals revealed Mary had only attended Lawrence during her freshman, sophomore, and the first half of her junior years. It seemed perfect. She needed to interrupt her education for an event during her second semester. I was born in April. I was told it was one of the few fragments of truth that hadn't been falsified on my second birth certificate. Now it was time to examine potential paternal candidates. Lawrence, being smaller, had only a handful of male professors during the late 1950s. Once again the annuals would be my archeological tool. As I closely examined the pictures, dissecting each facial feature, combing over every full-body view to analyze each body type, one emerged as an obvious choice: Professor Lennox. He appeared to be in his midthirties, with a wider hip structure and narrow shoulders. He must have been at least six feet tall, as the group shots of him depicted him taller than most. His deep-set eyes looked lighter, although the black-and-white photos available didn't confirm the blue mine exhibited. They looked to be a possible match. He had a thin upper lip, with a receding hairline similar to mine. The overall structure of his head and facial construction seemed similar as well. Not only did the physical manifestation convince me but also the academic accomplishments. By the time I was thirty-two, I had acquired two master's degrees. At forty-one I had nearly obtained my third. I loved education. It made sense that one of my biological parents held the same educational values. Despite these similarities, I needed further proof.

When I returned to the reference desk, I indicated my genealogical research was that of the Lennox family. Were there any other sources that might provide insight into Professor Lennox's tenure at Lawrence? The librarian advised me to complete an online search on the university's computer system. I was able to locate several articles on Professor Lennox, the last of which moved me closer to the assurance I was seeking. It seemed Professor Lennox left the university in the spring of 1959 to take a new teaching position at Rochester University in Rochester, New York. While it didn't disclose a reason, it did seem the change was rather abrupt. My certainty was growing. To me, it seemed likely Professor Lennox might have gotten caught in a scandal. Perhaps a younger woman, a former student, had come forward with her disclosure of an awkward pregnancy. Instead of bringing disgrace upon himself, he fled, saving his family from the wrath of a scorned lover and this conservative, exclusive community. While I recognized I had made many assumptions along the way, and any of my conclusions could be wrong, the ever-increasing multitude of the individual pieces of evidence seemed to increase the likelihood I was on the right path. The archives of the university held one more piece of potential evidence: Toward the end of Professor Lennox's stay at Lawrence, he made a speech that was recorded and put to rest in the audio section of the archives. As I listened, I heard a familiar tone to his voice. While the specific accent was distinctively northeastern, perhaps Western New York, something in the pitch and tone sounded similar to mine. At this point I was certain. I began my trip back home.

A NEW NORMALITY

My uncle Joe, Bob's youngest brother, and his wife, Jody, had invited us over for an evening supper. While I was happy to attempt reconnection with my extended adoptive family, like many of my previous encounters since the skeleton came out of the closet, the evidence of struggle emerged. Despite good intentions, many of us stumbled in our executions. Whether it was from not wanting to leave them out of this significant chapter of my life or simply to drag them back into my fractured state of lost identity, I found myself blurting every new discovery and revelation. This would inevitably lead to a termination of our conversations. Following my day of initial discovery, many of my relatives made periodic calls. Some offered apologies for the secret they had harbored for so long; others delivered explanations for why they hadn't come forth, even after my parents' deaths. But a few argued their own critical view of my rumored search for biological roots. How could I desecrate my parents' deaths? Didn't I understand it? My biological birth parents didn't want me then, and they certainly didn't want to know of me now. Why couldn't I simply leave the past where it belongs? At one holiday family gathering, Sylvia told me she had been cornered by one of my cousins, who decreed his disdain for my actions and questioned my sanity. My approval-seeking disposition, often common among late-discovery adoptees, began to give way to a coarser, angrier approach to social interaction. As the land mines of emotion erupted more frequently, the calls and invitations diminished.

In addition to my search, another obsession was finding out everything about adoptees. I devoured book after book, tailoring each new characteristic to my own unique needs. While a fair amount of literature existed on adoptees and adoption, there was virtually nothing on specifics unique to late-discovery adoptees. One book dedicated a paragraph to the subject, simply noting the devastating effects on those condemned to the affliction. My other source was the computer. My first find was Bastard Nation, the official self-proclaimed adoptee website. As they eagerly incorporated me into their world, I found a large supply of discussion boards, information sources, contacts, and action groups. Their main focus seemed to be the unfairness of the plight of the adoptee. Anger being the fuel, much energy seemed to focus on laws restricting access to identification information of the adoptee. This I did relate to; however, there was one striking difference between us. They knew from their earliest recollection of their birth status, whereas I spent forty-one years in the dark, unable to develop the ego needed to shield me from the harsh reality of my existence and accept my fate. Additionally, the site listed a link to another group devoted to the late-discovery adoptee. Finally, people I could relate to. As I ventured into their world and read different accounts, I realized I was not alone. While each story had its own unique twist and turn, the common thread of the fracturing discovery late in life seemed to validate my new complex reality. From early that first November, and ongoing for the next several years, these people formed my support group. Anger, betrayal, a loss of trust, and a universe of hunger for the next fragment of identity that would drift into life became my new state of normal. Like a life-sustaining drug, the comfort of my computer made me feel like that baby monkey clinging to its wire-mesh mother, with the formula bottle hanging in place of its mother's breast. She wasn't real, but only the computer could be trusted. Only the computer would be able to provide the emotional support needed as the ebbs and flows of my journey reshaped my identity. Throughout the years, the cast of characters on the website would emerge and then disappear for a while, most likely going periodically to the safe haven of denial. They would try to forget. Most were in the search process. Some were still trying to find the courage to search. Others had found answers but discovered that even though their dreams had come true it didn't necessarily mean the nightmare had ended. Like me, most had discovered a newfound capability: hurling spears of anger with deadly force.

One regrettable posting was that in response to Sue Donym. For months I enjoyed her insightful, spirited postings. They always seemed to cut to the chase and relay a meaning I echoed. At one point one of the other participants inquired as to whether she was of an Asian background.

For a long time I recognized her computer name to be one that hid her identity. Sue Donym simply was a disguise, created to shield her from the harsh reality she wanted to avoid. Perhaps she was aware of her birth status but didn't want to risk her adoptive family finding out about her awakening. The reason didn't matter. She was in a safe haven, and she shouldn't have to fear her exposure. I reached in my quiver, drew my arrow, and fired to the other participant. "Don't you realize Sue Donym is a fake name? It's a homophone for 'fake name.' She's still in denial." I hadn't seen postings from either again.

Similar spears of anger seemed to permeate other aspects of my life. Sylvia and I had become more distant. Frustrated, I entrenched. My recent discovery fueled a fear of rejection that seemed to explode in its magnitude. Driven by anger and distrust, I was starting to lose my faithfulness in her. Sex became a distant memory. Our relationship was on a path of disintegration. Little did I realize, my own loss of identity was infectious. I was no longer who she married, no longer who she shared the life-changing experience of bearing children. I had changed, and she didn't know me. She started to lose herself, yet she endured. I even questioned my own children. Were they really mine? I saw each of them born, and I even cut the cords that tied them to their mother's life, but no longer was I certain they were my issue. When I looked at them, I could see their mother, but not me. Grace I was certain of, but Madeline and Tony I questioned. Grace exhibited a similar facial mole pattern I had on my own face. Everything else fell into shades of gray. After all, I trusted everything I knew before, but so much was a lie.

My children also suffered. Grace witnessed the death of her grandfather, with most likely no recollection. But being three and four, Grace and Madeline each had their own faint memories of what the death of Grandmother Nicora meant. Tony was a newborn. When we moved to Wisconsin, I had taken a position at the local high school and was into my second year of teaching. After we moved back to Wisconsin, Sylvia agreed to stay home with Tony. It was a wager she lost. We both agreed in Minnesota that whoever was the first to be offered a teaching position would be the one to work that first year. I was the first to get a job. Once I discovered my birth status, I turned inward. Sylvia was in her first year back to work. She was in a constant state of exhaustion. My only concern was that of finding who I was. Investigation and contemplation eroded the time I had spent with them. The kids were losing their father. Even when I was with them, I really wasn't.

I had always been a social drinker. My parents were fairly heavy drinkers, but they never seemed to cross the fine line of being alcoholics. Their typical pattern was to have a stiff martini or two at five o'clock, followed by a few beers after supper. As far as I knew, it was the norm. At least, that's what I was taught. I thought I was doing better than them. I would occasionally put down a few drinks after work, but at least I didn't do it every day. But I began to find a new use for the spirits. It was a great way to dull the pain and rewrite every chapter of my life. After a few rum and Cokes, things seemed to take on a different glow. As I reevaluated all the chapters of my life based on my new understanding, the drinks seemed to act as a clarifier. New understandings were only a glass away. Our house was unique in that there was no inside access to the basement. I had been told the previous owner—and designer—decided he didn't want his kids getting into his tools, so he purposefully didn't put a staircase on the inside. For me, it offered the perfect getaway at home, where I could slowly drink my way into my own contemplative cocoon.

The holiday season was moving into full force. I long ago blended the remorseful feelings associated with the death of my father and those with the birth of my first child. Bittersweet is all I recall witnessing the birth of Grace in June, which amazed me, and my father's descent into death. He died in late 1993, just days before their wedding anniversary. Countless trips to Saint Luke's Hospital saw him turn more yellow each day. His liver was failing. Finally, fatally, his final transition was underway. Vague, illusive, disintegration robbed him of his final grasp of rational thought. What was once an ever-caring, committed father gave way to a shadow of a man uncertain of which way to turn. Life and death became something indistinguishable, as the process of death slowly gained control and inevitably won. Bittersweet had to meld with my new perspective. Now, in 2000, he was once again alive in my mind. I buried him. How can I have conversations with him if I buried him?

My mother had made the same fatal journey too. Fortunately, her death occurred during my summer break. My time with her was more complete. As an only child, the only available caregiver, the burden was on my shoulders. Her final days were spent in a long-term care facility. No less painful, my recollection in the aftermath of discovery revealed another revelation. She struggled to die. After repeated warnings of inevitable death from her caregivers, she seemed to continually rebound. What kept her alive? Why, after continual deathwatches, was she still alive? She had displayed the molding. She had exhibited the decreased kidney functions, yet she always seemed to rebound. Why? In the end, she continued to mutter something I couldn't understand. Later I realized her desperate mutterings were cries of her final confession. "You're adopted. You're adopted." Only after my discovery did I realize her final confession was incomprehensible to me at the time. Thankfully, I provided the comforting words that allowed her to let go. "I know. I understand." But I didn't. One of my biggest regrets during her final days occurred while I tried to comfort her. Her death had become inevitable. One day, while my daughters played by her bedside, I commented that through my genetic relay she and her sister lived on in her granddaughters. I hadn't a clue.

My students also saw a change. Most of my students are typically boys. Those who mature physically early and those who get in trouble are often those who end up in my classes. As a shop teacher, I realized they are who they are—the ones who need to see what an impulsive decision can lead to. I was honest from the beginning. I never lied. They were at an age and time when they could contribute to an unwanted pregnancy. They deserved to see what happens. They needed to understand the consequences. I could be their example. I could demonstrate the consequences of their impulses. And as always, they appreciated the cold reality of the truth. Given today's options, some of them had already dealt with the situation. Some of them were in the process of dealing with the situation.

Others were products of the situation. But all accepted it and moved on. Their view was back to the task at hand, as it was simply a cold, hard fact of life. Many of their realities were colder and harder. In some ways, the scrappy farm kids were the easiest to work with.

BACK TO THE SEARCH

The voice had been sluggish. First it was the explanation of the encroaching holiday season, followed by the potential budget cuts. But at last movement was in the picture again. My files had been located. It turned out that when the agency that processed my adoption folded all my records were sent to Green Bay. It should only be a few days until my files arrived in Madison. Then they could start the black out process. I still didn't tell the voice of my progress. Not only had I found my birth mother but perhaps even her partner. The voice would never understand. But isn't that the role of the bastard child—to do the unspeakable, to perform the unforgivable? In only six short weeks, I had mastered the role.

I contacted the University of Rochester. They sent me all I wanted to know about Professor Lennox. The information included his retirement, his death, even his kids. His death was a blow, but hell, it was just another disappointment on the long road of disappointments. Yes, I started to join the Bastard Nation in that cesspool of anger. When the package arrived, I was eager to look at more pictures of the paternal donor. Yet my hunger wasn't satisfied. I needed more. Maybe I could get more insight from his children. His wife was identified, but I couldn't find her. But as I conducted web searches, his daughter's name was a hit. Margaret Lennox was living in Portland, Oregon. Perhaps she could shed some light; perhaps she could help me find myself. I dialed the number and anxiously waited.

"Hello?"

"Hi, may I please speak with Margaret Lennox?" I responded.

"Speaking."

"My name is Fred Nicora. I think I may be related to you. But please hear me out and be open to what I have to say."

"Okay, but I'm not sure where this is going."

"About six weeks ago I found out I was adopted. I'm forty-one, and it was quite a shock."

"I'm sure it was."

"Yeah, you have no idea ..."

Nervously, I realized at any moment I might lose my chance with Margaret. I had rehearsed this in my head, but I found the words were now stuck in my throat. Insecurity ripped through my body. Fear had now replaced anger and hunger. Maybe I couldn't go through with this. But I had to. My mouth started to speak again. As I described my research, I slowly came to the point I feared most. Margaret had listened patiently as I skirted around the issue of paternity. But now the time had arrived.

"... Lawrence is where I think you enter the picture," I continued.

"I know Lawrence. My father taught there when I was young," Margaret interjected.

"I know. I think your father may be my father."

"Bah! I don't think so," Margaret blurted. "Well, maybe. No, he couldn't have. Although he was gone a lot."

Margaret had started her own dialogue. So far she hadn't hung up on me, and she seemed to be testing the thought. I proceeded to plead my case, based on my evidence of the physical features. Finally, I suggested I send her photos of not only myself but also of my children. Margaret agreed to take a look. She gave me her address and took my phone number. The case was still open. No verdict had been reached.

The following day I put together my package and sent it via overnight mail. Now I waited. What if she didn't call back? How many days should I give her? Hopefully she will be faster than the state. As I continued to wait, I realized it was the first time I had nothing to do. The ball was in her court. Each day felt like a month. Finally, three days after I sent my package, I returned home after school to see there was a message on our phone. It was Margret. She wanted me to call her back. Score! I dialed her number.

"Hi, Margaret?"

"Yes," she replied.

"This is Fred. You indicated I should give you a call."

"Oh, hi, Fred. I think you may be right."

"So you see a resemblance?" I questioned.

"I see some in you, but a lot in your children, especially your daughter Madeline. She looks a lot like me when I was growing up."

The conversation picked up its level of intensity. Margaret became an open book, flowing with all the answers to my endless string of questions. What was Professor Lennox like? What was my heritage? What was she like? What about her brothers? This was the first time in my life I was talking to a blood relative, besides my own children. Growing up an only child, I craved the thought of having a brother or sister. *Wow, this is what it feels like.* I was elated. Eventually, the conversation came to an end. Margaret made me promise I would not contact her mother. She said her health was frail, and she didn't want to see her upset. I agreed. As for her brother, she indicated their relationship was distant. I was more than welcome to contact him on my own, but she would rather not speak with him. She did tell me he was an artist—a glassblower in Rhode Island. He was divorced and had two daughters. Suddenly my family was growing. Now I even had new nieces. She also informed me that I was Scottish and German. Growing up in Milwaukee, I was familiar with the German side. I had already been part German. But the thought of being Scottish was something new. I loved the thought of being Scottish. Before I had been Romanian, Polish, and German. Scottish seemed to fit better. We agreed to keep in contact. She indicated she wanted to keep abreast on my research and findings. I made her aware I was still waiting on the state.

Among the many other missed clues was my appearance. My father was Romanian. Both of his parents came from a small town in Romania called Dava, although his older sister always argued we were really Hungarian. At the time of their ancestors' departure, Dava was actually located on the Hungarian side of the border. I was a gypsy. I, of course, sided with my father and stuck with the Romanian argument. To me, the only significant aspect of Romania was its tie to Transylvania and Count Dracula. It made for great Halloween costume potential. Following the death of my mother, I decided to dedicate my upper bicep to my Romanian heritage. Ink was etched into an armband to celebrate Romania's Roman past. A rich Roman engraving circled my upper arm to remind me of his blood flowing through my veins. In addition to my Romanian blood, my mother's Polish-German heritage set my genealogy in eastern Europe. In retrospect, my mother looked Polish, as did the rest of her family, and my father and his family looked Romanian. Both had darker hair. My mother had brown eyes, and my father had blue. While my blue eyes still held together as I learned about the dominant gene patterns in tenth-grade biology class, my blond hair was a bit of a stretch. My other problem was my body size. I was taller and thicker than both my parents— by a lot. They both looked eastern European. I did not. The Nordic side to the Scots seemed to fit much better.

Once again I had things to research. I immersed myself in my new-found Scottish identity. One trip to Borders, a nearby bookstore, resulted in an artillery of research materials. My prized Lennox heritage even contained its own tartan plaid and coat of arms. At the next Scottish Highland games, I would buy a kilt. Maybe I should learn to play the bagpipes. Cocktail table books proudly displayed my latest discoveries. I also flooded our house with modern Gaelic music. Ashley MacIsaac, an angry Gael from Nova Scotia, performed with an intensity that seemed to parallel my passion for the Scots, and it fit my identity as a bastard. Another artist, Steve McDonald, sang ballads of the Scots being forced from their home to settle the new world. The songs touched a nerve. I, too, had been forced from my home with no recourse. Suddenly I once again began to feel hope. I was finding a new identity.

Sylvia also enjoyed my newly discovered roots. She came from a long line of Cavenaughs, a name full of a rich Irish heritage. Sylvia long ago declared her admiration of the British Isles and in particular Ireland. Now we were neighbors. Our distance started to lessen. Perhaps it was something I found, or maybe it was just that I was happy I had found something. Unfortunately, damage had already taken its toll, and our road to marital recovery still was on a fragile path. But at least the decline was redirected. My children also became fascinated with their Scottish roots. We had recently attended a holiday parade in Milwaukee, and they wondered if I was going to get a skirt. "Kilt," I barked out. "It's a kilt." I learned kilts were actually a functional piece of clothing used to travel through the wet Scottish bogs. Yes, we all embraced the newly discovered sides of our identities.

I got the call from the state. My blacked-out file would be completed tomorrow. While I was excited to see what it contained, I was fairly certain I had already put the pieces of the puzzle together, and I knew what the picture looked like. Nevertheless, I didn't want to wait the two to three days it would take to arrive in the mail. So I asked what time their office closed. She indicated 4:30 p.m. I knew it would be tight, but I figured if I left right after school was dismissed, 2:47 p.m., I could make the hour-and-a-half ride to Madison just in time to have the file in my hands. I informed her of my plan, and we agreed to meet the following day between 4:15 p.m. and 4:30 p.m. Once again time seemed to move at a snail's pace. At last my school day had come to a close. I beat the school buses out of the parking lot, and I was on my way. It seemed like I was making good time. I decided to cut through the center of the state, as opposed to heading down through Milwaukee and then west to Madison via the interstate. The mileage was greater going through Milwaukee, but it took about the same amount of time, as taking the back roads was a more direct route. I feared I might hit traffic in Milwaukee. But once I hit Horicon, the unthinkable happened. A train was stalled on the tracks. Ten, fifteen, then twenty minutes crept by. I couldn't believe my luck. I had waited nearly forty-two years to read this file, and it would be this fucking train parked in Horicon, Wisconsin, that would delay my date with destiny. Finally, the train had cleared the road; I realized there was no way I could make it to Madison by 4:30 p.m. It was now 3:55 p.m., and I still had at least another forty-five minutes. I called Madison from a nearby gas station. I knew the stop would eliminate any hope of to Madison by my deadline, but I thought if I asked, given my circumstances, someone might wait for me or agree to meet me with the file. Unfortunately, I was wrong. The futility of the situation sunk in. I decided I would call in sick the following day. It was the only day I would have missed as a result of my discovery. I felt it was justified, given the magnitude of the situation. I requested they hold the file, and I would pick it up the following day. They agreed.

When the alarm went off the following morning, I couldn't believe the day was here. The punitive actions of Lady Luck the day before took an about-face. Tony, my youngest, woke up saying he didn't feel well. With Tony, I never could tell fact from fiction. From the day he stepped into kindergarten, he hated school. It was a surprise to both my wife and I. While neither of us were great students growing up, we both still wanted to go to school. Tony was different. For the first couple of years, every morning was a battle involving tears and bribery. Eventually, Tony accepted his fate, and the resistance lessened, eventually going away. But both Sylvia and I had grown so accustomed to the litany of excuses that we would always seek physical proof. A fever, vomit, or blood was the litmus test. If he didn't produce, off to school he went. But today was different. "I'll stay home with him," I insisted. This, too, was a deviation from our usual pattern. Neither Sylvia nor I liked missing a day of teaching. Our main fear was of getting a substitute who allowed for the total destruction of any form of order in the classroom or battling the endless cries of "I gave my assignment to the sub. He must have lost it." It just wasn't worth it. Both Sylvia and I kept track of who was home last and whose turn it was that day. With three younger children, those days were all too common. But today I gladly took the high road. Besides, now I didn't have to call in sick and risk having word make it back to my school that I wasn't really ill. The teaching profession enjoys many days off, but the flexibility of those days is that of granite. Tony and I were on the road by eight. If everything went right, we would arrive in Madison by nine thirty. This time I took the interstate. By nine, we were twenty miles from Madison. I made my call to announce my anticipated arrival. Everything seemed to be in place.

Soon I was in front of 1 West Wilson Street, the home of the Department of Health and Family Services, Division of Children and Family Services. It was such a long name. Even with all those words, it didn't seem to fit me. It did bring to mind a point highlighted in one of the adoption books I read. Basically, it suggested that everyone has empathy for an orphan child, yet the day the child turns eighteen they are no longer considered an orphan. Yes, we all have to grow up, but facts of birth status don't change the same day one turns eighteen. In a way, the title of the department seemed to be saying, "If you're an adult, go ask someone else."

We made it up to the third floor. I informed the receptionist that I was here to see Jaycee, the name of the voice. When Jaycee appeared, I was surprised. An energetic yet assuring greeting seemed to help my mind feel relaxed. Jaycee escorted Tony and I back to her cubical, where she promptly handed me the envelope. I asked if I could fill out the request for seeking my birth mother's identification. She strongly suggested I read the file first. She indicated many times the file contained information that helped generate a letter with a greater likelihood of a favorable response. If I wanted, however, I could fill out the application to start the process and send her the letter once I had developed it. I did as she suggested and headed down to the car.

As we walked down the stairs, back to the first floor, I felt the tension in my body erupt. My original plan was to drive home before opening the envelope to read its contents in the safe haven of my house. But with each step, I felt the tension and anxiety build. I thought I was on the right path with my own research. How could I have been wrong? There were several assumptions, but the professor had to be a hit. Not only had I gotten him through the path of my mother but even his own daughter agreed. The physical evidence was overwhelming. I must be right. There were just too many coincidences for my conclusions to be wrong. Even beyond physical features was the pursuit of academic achievement. Professor Lennox had earned a PhD earlier in life. While I didn't have a PhD, I had already completed two master's degree programs and was nearly finished with my third. In addition to those similarities with the professor was the timing of Mary's and the professor's departure from Lawrence. The fact she was the only candidate who went to a four-year university and wasn't married by the time I was born all seemed to lead down the path I followed. It all seemed to fit into place. I did good research. I checked my findings with those around me. Sylvia thought I was right. I must be right. So why, then, was I so nervous about the envelope? What did I fear?

Once we got to the first-floor lobby, the tension felt as if I was being stretched apart. I couldn't take it any longer. I had to see what was inside. It was thicker than I thought it should be. I assumed it would simply be a fact sheet that would read like a pornographic rap song with most of the words deleted. All the relevant information would be missing. All substance would be blacked out.

"Tony, let me see what's in here." I started to rip open the top of the manila letter-sized envelope.

"Dad, no, let's go. I'm hungry," bellowed Tony, his frustration reverberating off the polished marble walls.

"This will be quick. I promise."

"I'm hungry." His impatience was growing.

"I'll get you a Happy Meal if you just give me a minute," I pleaded.

"Okay, but hurry."

As its contents emerged, I saw the initial fact sheet I anticipated, which, just as I suspected, contained many more black streaks than readable lines. Additionally, the photocopy was very dark, and difficult to read. But behind it was a treasure. It seemed to be some sort of diary. Carefully typed pages logged and documented my biological mother's days during her pregnancy. As I scanned further, I observed it was completed by a social worker. It must have been Mary's caseworker, who was working for the agency as she was processed.

"Okay, Dad, let's go!" Tony bellowed.

"Tony, just wait. We'll go soon."

"But you promised. I'm hungry."

I knew from past experience that my forty-one years of patient waiting would be an unworthy opponent to my four-year-old's desire for McDonald's. I stuffed the contents back in the envelope and worked my way through the Madison streets back to our van. Maybe, just maybe, if I went through the drive-through I could grab some time in the parking lot. My appetite had also swung into full force, as I didn't take time to eat breakfast that morning. But it nowhere equaled my ravenous hunger for the contents of what lay in the envelope. What else was in there? Would it hint at the identity of Professor Lennox? Would clues remaining between the dark black streaks describe what I remembered from my trip to Lawrence? Would it tell me about Mary's family? God, I hoped there was a McDonald's close.

At last it was in sight. It was before the noon rush, so the line was fairly short. One McNuggets Happy Meal and one Quarter Pounder with cheese were acquired, and it was off to the first available parking space. I calculated I had about fifteen minutes of reading time before the impatient nagging would resume, and we would be on our way back home. I would make the best of the time available. My mental hunger would supersede the needs of my physical hunger. I could eat and drive, not read and drive. Once I fulfilled my duties as the carhop, I quickly resumed reading my file. The fact sheet disclosed that I was Norwegian, German, Irish, and English. That didn't seem right. Where was the Scottish? Further investigation indicated my mother was a fourth-grade teacher. This also didn't support her student status. Maybe she graduated early, or maybe it meant she was student teaching. I wasn't sure, but it made me start to feel uneasy. My biological father's occupation was a construction worker. Now I was really confused. My aunt said he was a professor. This wasn't right. Did the state mess up again? I didn't get it. I continued to read the social worker's documents. My mind was becoming clouded. Was I wrong? How could I be wrong?

"What's wrong, Dad?" Tony inquired.

He could see the confusion on my face. Four-year-olds can be so insightful.

"We're not Scottish," I responded. It was the only response that popped into my head that I thought would make sense to him.

"Oh. Can we go?"

"Sure."

This was a blow. Once again it seemed as if I was the only one with the misunderstanding. But how? It was all so confusing. At this point I realized I would really need to comb through the information. It would take longer than a happy meal stop in a McDonald's parking lot. It was time to make the trip home. It was back to plan A. I would continue my way back to my house, where I could digest the rest of the file in the comfort of my home. It seemed like a safe place to be. We drove on.

Tony fell asleep in the back seat. Just as my first walk on the beach drew me deep into a form of internal self-reflective babble, the ninety-minute ride home had the same effect. Once again I was alone with my thoughts. The scraps of identity I had started to sew together had unraveled into a pile of meaningless pieces of thread. It was garbage, something to be disposed of. It was something to be filed. But what went wrong? Where did I turn down the wrong path? I found a glimmer of light in the realization that for the first time in my life at least I was dealing with cold, hard fact. Even though the most trusted document in all our lives, our birth certificates, had simply been a fabricated set of lies, I still believed I needed to trust its author, the state. I had to. They had better information than I did, and I needed to move forward. I had to believe what they were telling me this time. Fool me once, shame on me. Fool me twice, I must be adopted. That was my newest revelation. Now I was back to square one. Beyond this reality, I started to realize I had been lost in a world of self-pity. Why me? It was my newest battle cry. I didn't ask for this, or did I? For forty-one years I had been part of a typical American nuclear family, with no significant public issues. Some would have dismissed Sylvia's documentation of Lydia's comment, simply stating she doesn't know what she's talking about. Perhaps some wouldn't have even cared. But for some reason that just wasn't in my constitution. I couldn't let it go. It couldn't be unchecked. The answer had to be found. With that newest revelation, I made a decision: I needed to move on. So what! I was wrong. Maybe my biggest fault—and cause for all this self-inflicted pain—was my impatience. Had I just waited for the state to reveal their latest version of the truth, I could have avoided all this Lennox mess. *Oh shit! Margaret. How am I going to tell Margaret? I'll wait until I have a name. If things go well, it should only be a few days.* We were talking every four or five days, so maybe I could just put off my apology until I was certain.

At last we were almost home. Tony had been awake since we passed by Milwaukee. I just didn't trust that back-road route anymore. Hell, I didn't trust much anymore. Yes, the anger was starting to creep back. It was midafternoon, and soon Sylvia and the rest of the kids would be home. Quiet, inward, reflective reading time was impossible when the Nicora household was in full force. My plan: I would stop and get Tony a movie on the way home and have at least an hour to digest the rest of the file by myself. It was a plan. It was executed. It worked.

CHAPTER 2

THE SEARCH MUST GO ON

November 2000

We were home. Tony was engrossed in his *Pokémon* movie, and I had time to read. This called for a Scotch and water. It seemed so ironic. Here I was going to find out everything about me that wasn't a Scot, yet I went for the Scotch. It was just another ironic twist in my life. In my second life, the first irony was my birth date. I had been born on April Fools' Day. When I first accessed the late-discovery adoptee website, I discovered their mascot was the court jester, the April fool. Not only had I pegged the core meaning of what the site was about but even their mascot seemed to be tailored to my unique identity, or lack thereof.

Now was the time to find out about me. I began to read. Included in the manuscript was a picture of me and my mother. While the picture looked vaguely familiar, I realized I had never seen the picture before. I had only seen a similar picture in our family's photo album. Only now did I realize it was a series of photos whose purpose was to fulfill the needs of the state. The picture I had seen was one of a series to complete the adoption process. In the envelope of my blacked-out file was another picture from the same series, along with a copy of a handwritten letter from my biological mother. Her letter documented her gratefulness that the process had delivered her boy into a caring, wanting family. It also thanked my family for providing the picture, which I now believed concluded the process of surrendering her child. It was dated July 8, 1959. It all seemed so formulated. It summarized the psychological thought of the time. There was a process and remedy for everything. It was a simple solution.

The rest of the file was fascinating. It not only told me of what happened throughout the process of her pregnancy but it also documented her feelings and views of what happened as well. In addition, it provided background about where she was from and who she was. An example of one paragraph from the text is as follows:

██████ is the oldest. Then comes ██████ born ██████40, who is a freshman and the University of Wisconsin in ██████ ██████ born ██████41 and ██████ born ██████43, both of whom are high school students. Mr.██████ is postmaster at ██████ Mrs.██████ has been a housewife throughout the marriage.

While the text may be frustrating to someone with full knowledge of their past, to me it provided valuable insight into a past I had sought for so long. To me, it was a gold mine. I knew so much more than I did before. While I was no longer a Scot, I knew more than I did before. Yes, it was similar to that edited Walmart version of a life, but once again it gave me something to hold on to. It was like being caught in a storm at sea. I didn't focus on the fact there wasn't much to hold on to, only the fact the one rock I clung to kept me breathing.

Initially, I paged trough the file. It contained approximately twenty pages of single-spaced manually typed text, each page marred with the periodic black marker streaks. The amount of information surprised me. The first entry was dated December 23, 1958. She was described as rather sheepish. My biological mother was sheepish. It didn't seem like a very good start. It further stated she was a schoolteacher in her local community who had gotten pregnant by the alleged father (AF) after she had been dating him for "sometime." I was relieved. At least it seemed I was conceived in some sort of a meaningful relationship. It also struck me that even if I was able to get her to disclose her identity the closest I would get to identify my biological father would be the alleged father. But then it dawned on me: Isn't that what everyone lives with? We all grow up under the assumption our fathers are our biological fathers. It's only as we mature and see aspects of our fathers in us do we become certain. The entry went on to describe money the AF owed her. While dating, he was working on the construction of a school in her community. But it seemed his work was sporadic, as he didn't work for one construction company but took work as it became available. The previous October was the last time he had been working. It seemed unlikely she would ever receive the $1,800 he owed her, even though he agreed to pay her back. She had trusted him, but now looked at her trust as foolishness. The report outlined a plan to have her placed into a work wage home for the duration of her pregnancy, close to a hospital and clinic. This would keep her out of sight from relatives and friends, as her pregnancy became more apparent. Such was one of the few paths available to wayward girls in the 1950s.

Subsequent entries described her final days prior to her placement in the work wage home, preparing for her stay in Milwaukee. Both of her parents, my grandparents, were described as supportive. While her father seemed to be rather matter-of-fact about her condition, her mother was described as seeming hurt and embarrassed. My biological mother was depicted as talking freely about the situation, but occasionally seemed

37

to be confused and on the verge of tears. It made me realize how difficult this time was for her, and how difficult it must have been for other women who found themselves in similar situations. It went on to discuss her feelings about teaching. It seemed she was drawn to problem children, especially one little boy who was "trying" in his behavior. She attributed his struggles as the result of being from a poor family. It seemed she had her own revelation at this point. She could see she was also describing the AF. Already I felt a connection. The students she seemed to be drawn to were similar to those with whom I enjoyed working.

Much of the text was centered on the AF. Toward the end of the pregnancy, the social worker was looking at pictures she carried with her. Among them were those of her sisters, along with one of the AF. While she allowed the social worker to keep the pictures of her sisters, she insisted that he could look at but must return the one she had of the AF. Given she was surrendering her baby, this wouldn't be to show the child later in life who the father was. It became apparent: she still had feelings for him. But she also seemed to be concerned that he never had access to the child. During a conversation, around the time she first disclosed her pregnancy to him, he indicated they could marry, but he was certain it would result in a divorce. This seemed to be a less than romantic proposal. He further indicated that his grandparents or aunt could raise the baby. During their relationship, he disclosed that one of his parents had died as the result of an accidental shooting when he was young, and his grandparents raised him, with some time being spent at an aunt's house. He further confided that this was the cause of much of the unhappiness in his life. The last thing she wanted to see was this baby in the same situation as the AF. She was assured he wouldn't have access to the baby.

Toward the end of her pregnancy, the report focused on postdelivery plans. She indicated she was thinking of moving out of state. A close friend of hers was teaching in California. She knew she would miss her family, but she needed distance from this whole situation. Her social worker was leaving, and her case would be handled by a new social worker.

The delivery was expected within the next two weeks. Throughout the pregnancy, she had been receiving periodic letters from the AF's grandparents. He had disappeared. She responded by indicating the AF and her had broken up, and she was unaware of his whereabouts. As she contemplated disclosure of the pregnancy to them, her family discouraged her. It stirred up recollection of the money he owed her, and they thought at this point they should forget about it and move on. She did as they advised.

On April 1, 1959, she delivered a baby boy: 7 pounds, 3 ounces, 19.5 inches long, at 5:45 a.m. These facts remained consistent on both of my birth certificates. The new social worker summarized the work of the previous social worker. Most of the information remained similar, with the exception of her physical appearance. He commented that she displayed a medical condition, neurofibromatosis. This was the first time in forty-one years I was aware of any factual genetic medical conditions in my biological roots. When my adoptive father died, however, it was from colon cancer. As I was considered part of a high-risk population, I received colonoscopies, a very uncomfortable procedure, every other year from the time I was thirty-three until the time of my discovery. As the chapters of my discovery unfolded, there did not seem to be any colon cancer in either branch of my biological family. I haven't had another colonoscopy since.

Neurofibromatosis is a fifty-fifty disease. Either you've got it, or you don't. Myself and my half sister Katie didn't. My other half brother Tim and my other half sister Jane did. Unfortunately, Jane died before I had a chance to meet her. She died at the age of twenty, many years before I had the chance to meet her. From what everyone told me, she was a dear, engaging, energetic soul. Even though I never had the chance to meet her, I miss her.

The entries also described what happened after I was born. She struggled with thoughts of giving her baby away. Following her delivery, one of her roommates was on her third child out of wedlock. It didn't seem like a big deal. It happened. Why should this time be any different? Another was having her second. She was also going to keep this one. It all seemed so confusing. She made her choice. Why were there suddenly other options? There weren't, especially for girls like her. Her baby would be surrendered. It was what was expected. She followed the rules. Even in the end, her entries indicated she would have rather kept the baby, but she felt she had no choice. Societal norms of the time ruled over preference, she would follow through with the adoption. It was what she was supposed to do. She needed to be a proper girl again. She lost her baby.

The final entrees of the file dealt with the legal surrendering of her baby. Court dates and testimonies sealed my fate. I was gone forever. I was no longer hers. The fate of her child was now in the hands of the state. They would decide where I would go. The state was my new parent. She agreed. I was an orphan. It was final.

I made it through the file before Sylvia and the girls returned home. I lived a new life and managed to make it back to my current reality before they arrived. Suddenly I was back in my old world. It was a world without a past, a world with no foundation. But I felt different. I had information. More fragments of my past appeared. The girls were screaming, and Tony's movie was over. It was time to live in the present. The 1950s were gone again. It was the year 2000. I needed to snap back to reality. It was hard. But I did.

I had done as Jaycee suggested and read the file. It was time to write my letter. While at school the following day, much of my time was spent mulling over the words I would write. How do I write a letter compelling enough to allow me to find out my identity? My fate lied in the few words I would choose. I already knew so much about her, but that didn't seem to matter. She had to believe I was worthy. Could I live up to the expectations she had envisioned for the last forty-one years? I had accomplished so much, but was it enough? She discarded me once before. Would she do it again? I just didn't know. During my first-hour preparation period, I called Jaycee. Did she have any recommendations of how I should write my letter? She had seen this process unfold before. I wanted to know if she saw any patterns to successful letters versus letters that failed. Jaycee was helpful. She cautioned me that my letter was only one of the determining factors that would affect my biological mother's deci-sion. In many cases, these women had moved on and had established new lives for themselves, often not disclosing their past to their current part-ners or subsequent children. My current dilemma was one they buried long ago—in my case, nearly forty-two years. She also noted that even if she rejected my first letter and had to wait for my next window she could act in the interim. Maybe she would just need some time to digest it. Maybe she would need time to reveal her previous life to her husband and children. But she further indicated most of the letters she had delivered resulted in a reunion. She also had some helpful strategies. She suggested I keep it fairly short. I didn't want to bog her down in details that didn't specifically deal with the situation at hand. As I probed further, she sug-gested I keep it under two hundred words. She also indicated I should provide information that would result in her wanting to know more. Let her know about my children, but don't tell her too much. I thought it seemed like grandchildren were good bait. I appreciated her help. I got to work. I wrote the following letter:

> I am forty-one, married with three children, living in a small Wisconsin town where I teach high school, teaching technical education. Prior to being a teacher, I was an architect specializ-ing in Healthcare Architecture. I was raised as an only child, in a suburban Milwaukee home, by two loving parents. Thank you for the gift of life.
>
> On Sunday, October 22, 2000, I "acciden-tally" found out I was adopted through a slip of the tongue. Both of my parents had passed away before I found out about my adoption. Most of my living relatives know very little about my adoption. I am curious about who I am for myself, and my family. I am not angry and do not wish anyone harm. I am open to finding out

anything I can, at whatever level you are comfortable with. I will respect your decision regarding my degree of confidentiality. Please help me.

I called Jaycee. It was ready. I was ready. I sent her the letter. I waited.

The phone rang. It had only been about an hour, but she already had an answer. She made the call and communicated my message. I felt that since it was such a short turn around I had a fifty-fifty chance of success. Either she couldn't divulge my history because of her own secret past, or her key would unlock the secrets of my past. If she decided it was acceptable for me to find out my identity, it would be my turn. I would be given her name and phone number. I answered.

"Hello?"

"Hi, Fred. It's Jaycee."

"Hi, Jaycee. What did she say?"

"She wants to know you."

"What?" Of course I knew what it meant, but I was struggling on what to say.

"She said you should call her. Her name is Maureen Nelson, and she wants you to call her."

I couldn't believe it. I was originally wrong about my mother—twice. But it didn't matter. The only thing that mattered was that I finally knew. For the first time I heard the name of my biological mother. *God, Chic, I miss you.* Chic was my mother. Holy shit—that's the name of my mother! The emotions were overwhelming. I couldn't believe it. This was my mother. It had been so long. Why didn't I know? For the first time in my life I knew who my mother was. I knew so much about her, and she knew so little about me. Jaycee was right. Her strategy paid off. But why did it? Why did I have to beg her in order to find out who I was? Maybe the Bastard Nation was right. But I didn't care. She was my answer. She was the one who could provide the rest of the answers. Just as I had to yield to the state, once again I had to yield to my mother. Only she could provide the answers to my questions. I had to play the game.

I was still at school. But I couldn't wait. I couldn't wait until I got to the safety of my home. I had to know now. The school day had ended; the students had left. I dialed the number.

"Hi, Maureen. This is Fred."

"Fred, hi."

"I think I'm your son."

Her voice was comforting. It made me feel at ease in a motherly sort of way. Of course it did—she was my mother. How could it feel any other way? But who could understand? I certainly didn't. My emotions had reached a new high. I had become an emotional junky, ever seeking a new high. I loved my mother; I buried my mother. But this woman was my mother. It all made sense, but none of it made sense. I didn't get it. We talked, and I absorbed new information. I listened to every word as if they were the only words I ever heard. This was the first time I was talking to her. I buried her, but I was talking to her. Before we talked further she made me promise no one would ever know she was my mother. She was embarrassed she had gotten into this situation. Her friends and neighbors must never know I was her son. I was an embarrassment. I agreed. No one would ever know I was her son.

The biggest revelation was that of my previous name. Maureen told me she named me Steven Walter. I had a previous name for the first eight weeks of my life. I never knew I was a Steven. I felt so many emotions, yet logic regained control. I was after facts. "Tell me who I am" was the gist of my dialogue. Who are you? Do I have brothers and sisters? And finally, the potentially fatal question, who is my father? Once again Lady Luck was on my side. Maureen was an open book. My father was Don Brookshier. Inevitably, it was time for another leap. I felt shaky. Would she agree to meet me in person? My letter promised I would allow for whatever level of contact she wanted. I needed to abide by my word.

"Would it be all right to come and visit you?"

"That would be nice. I would like to meet you."

Once again the junky got his fix. I couldn't have asked for a better result. Arrangements were made. I had a day off approaching. I would drive the ninety minutes to meet her in her home. After she agreed to meet me, she indicated she had neurofibromatosis, and I should be aware of her appearance. I indicated I was aware of it from the file and had completed some research to understand what it was. Just as soon as the discussion began, it seemed to end. But little did she know, it wasn't what she answered but how she answered the questions.

The next week was one of the longest of my life. I had learned my lesson in patience. It was also time to talk to Margaret. Only did Margaret's graciousness become apparent as I disclosed my findings. Not only did she remain supportive but indicated she had enjoyed our conversations and actually wished I really was her half brother. I was embarrassed but justified my intrusion into her life based on the constrictions placed on me by the adoption laws. Yes, I would try to be more patient as my own discoveries continued. I made my apologies and agreed, as she asked that I keep her informed about my journey. Unfortunately, I did not live up to my side of that bargain.

HE'S DOWN UNDER

As I now had a name, I could start to look for my biological father. I had other friends who were adopted. One, Bob, was an architect I worked with when we lived in Minneapolis. I called him when I had the name of Don Brookshier. When I worked with Bob, I recalled he had spent much time searching for his biological mother. His search was complicated by the fact his adoption was completed in Philadelphia, Pennsylvania. Searching across state lines came with another set of complications. Bob knew all the search tools, and he would have insight. I was right. The Social Security Death Index (SSDI) was the first place to start. It's hard to say whether finding the name on the SSDI was a blessing or a curse. A name only appeared on the SSDI once someone had died. But at least I would know. Bob also had an interesting insight. Of all his friends he had told about his adoption, I was the one who showed the most interest. I was the only one who would periodically inquire about his search.

Another adopted friend was Janice. Janice was Tad's boyfriend. Tad also worked with me in Minneapolis. While Sylvia and I were together in Minneapolis, before we had our children, we spent much time with Tad and Janice. Tad was very laid back, but Janice had a very intense personality. Early in our friendship, she made it clear she was adopted. Sylvia and I often joked that Janice might be the undisclosed daughter of Jackie Kennedy. A beautiful woman, her physical appearance had a striking resemblance to Jackie. I remembered Janice from my years in architecture school in Milwaukee. She was a few years ahead of me, and as underclassmen often do, I looked up to her. Whether it was my admiration for her or the fact she was adopted, I constantly made excuses to Sylvia for her angry behavior, explaining, "But, Sylvia, she's had a hard life. She's adopted." Both situations were years before I was aware of my own birth status. I didn't realize it at the time, but those were actually other clues.

I searched the SSDI. Don was listed. He died in 1993—the same year as my father.

A VISIT TO MAUREEN

The day had arrived. I left my house armed with photos, my file, and the directions to her home. During our phone discussion, she seemed interested in where I grew up, who my parents were, and what I had done with my forty-one years. Every decision I made that morning was centered on what Maureen might think. I considered what I wore and even which vehicle I brought. Would it be the family van or my pickup truck? The truck won. It was more me. I also warned her of my appearance. Male-pattern baldness took its toll in my twenties and thirties. During the final year of my mother's life, while I was making the weekly six-hour commute on weekends to spend time with her, I decided to shave the few remaining strongholds from my head. I had become a chrome dome, complete with a diamond stud earring. As a way to deal with the stress of watching her disintegration, I also became obsessed with weight lifting. The physical release of the stress seemed to help. Some might have turned to food, some to alcohol, but I resorted to exercise. It was one of the better decisions in my life. But by the time the year had ended, I had bulked up my six-foot frame to 240 pounds, with very little body fat. The end result was a mix between Jesse Ventura and Stone Cold Steve Austin. My middle school students at that time nicknamed me Stone Cold. How would she respond to this all-star wrestler at her door?

As I approached her home, I felt my anxiety levels rise. Did I really want to walk down this path? Was I ready for what lie ahead? Ready or not, I had to go. Once again my constitution ruled. Her home was in a quiet residential neighborhood lined with trees, planted I estimated sometime in the late 1950s. Its light blue aluminum siding, complete with a white wrought iron fence, emulated the perfect grandmother's home. It looked so peaceful. I parked the truck, rang her doorbell, and waited. As the door opened, and I caught my first look at my biological mother, an array of thoughts and emotions filled my head. It's hard to recall which thoughts came first, but I knew my mind was traveling at the speed of light. At first I didn't see any striking similarity between Maureen, myself, or my own biological offspring. But then I thought, *Maybe Tony has her eyes. Is that what Madeline's nose will look like when she grows up? She's shorter than I imagined. I thought my height was one of the clues I missed earlier. I hope I'm not scaring her off.* I could hear myself delivering a socially acceptable greeting, but was I really making any sense? Insecurity ripped through my body.

Maureen was very welcoming. We hugged at the door, and she brought me into her living room. Pictures of her family decorated the room. While I tried to keep eye contact, as I knew was the correct thing to do, my eyes were scouring the room. This room was equivalent to that of the unearthing of an ancient burial site. It was a rich archeological find, which described a world long ago lost. She offered me something to drink, which I responded to, indicating a glass of water would be fine. When she went to her kitchen, I quickly rose and continued to examine my find. The piano top was a gold mine. Several pictures sat on the top of the piano, with a wide assortment hanging above it. Who were they? Were these all my siblings or cousins or merely family friends? When she returned with my water, my curiosity was evident by my fixed gaze on the pictures. "That's Katie. She lives in Brookfield. They moved back—oh, I want to say five years ago. This is my grandson Alex."

The awkwardness of the preface was over. We had begun the main body of the text.

The next two hours were filled with so many answers, which led to so many more questions. I realized I wasn't the only one with questions. It was apparent her ordeal, nearly forty-two years ago, was still part of her present. She indicated the adoption laws changed in the early 1980s, which allowed for the current system of allowing adoptees to seek contact, using the state as an intermediary. At that time her husband was still alive. He didn't know. She believed and feared I might have surfaced then, but she never received the phone call. She thought at that time, she wouldn't have volunteered her identity. She didn't think Tim Sr., her husband, would have taken it well. But as time went on she eventually accepted the fact she may never know what happened to me. Every April first she wondered. Was I even alive? She said there was a sense of relief when the call came.

She described each of her children. Katie was the oldest. She was a very successful woman who bore her only grandchild. Her husband, Sean, had colon cancer, a disease I knew all too well. She appreciated Katie's close proximity but resented Sean's lack of ability to work. She stated that all he did was complain. Katie was followed by Timmy Jr., an engineer. He also had neurofibromatosis, but Maureen indicated he had really made something of his life. Jane was the youngest. She was a very talented musician. Jane died of a brain tumor in her early twenties. Her death was the most difficult memory of Maureen's life. Children shouldn't die before their parents. She was very proud of her children. She also indicated she told Katie and Tim about my call. She thought she had told them about my birth following the death of their father. Katie remembered, but Tim didn't. He was struggling with my existence. She thought with some time he would adjust.

Eventually, it was time for pictures. There were many pictures of her sisters. To me, they didn't look like they were even related to each other. Maureen also showed me pictures of her parents. She commented on how supportive they were during the time she was pregnant with me, and what a difficult period it was for her and her family. I felt her pain. She searched but couldn't find a picture of Don, my biological father. She thought she had it somewhere, but that was so many years ago. Maybe she got rid of it when her husband died. I told Maureen about finding Don on the SSDI and what it meant. She paused, sighed, and indicated it was a relief. Finally, her past was behind her. Before I left she told me it was my eyes. My eyes looked exactly like Don's.

I told her my own research had led me down the wrong path; however, she was surprised how close I had come to the truth. Mary Miller was a friend of hers. They were in the same high school graduating class. What I didn't factor into the equation was the teaching license requirements of the time. Maureen went to a three-year certificate program. My other revelation at the time was that of my aunt's disclosure of my biological father being a professor. I reasoned my father had somehow misunderstood a parent being in education for that of my biological father being a professor.

It was time for our first meeting to end. It felt natural for it to end. I had met my biological mother for the first time, and now I knew who she was. Many meetings were to follow. Some of those meetings were with my family, which included her grandchildren, my children, and Katie's children. At last I found some answers.

The trip back home was full of reflection. What would my life have been like had she decided to keep me? She seemed like a nice woman; I'm sure she would have been a good mother. But I realized should she have kept me, I wouldn't have been raised by Nic and Chic. I loved Nic and Chic, and I missed them. I wished I could have been able to share this chapter of my life with them. They loved me—that I knew. They gave me the best life they could. They decided not to share the secret of my birth status with me, but that was part of who they were and a philosophy of the time. I also thought of each of my newfound siblings. What were they like? Would I get to know them? It was up to Maureen. I made a deal. I would live with the consequences. If she would allow me to find out who my brother and sister were, I would pursue. If not, I would have to live with my side of the agreement.

Maureen indicated it was all right to contact Katie, but I should give Tim some time. She gave me Katie's number, and I called her when I got home. We talked for some time. She recalled that Maureen told her of my existence, but she couldn't remember exactly when it occurred. She was surprised Tim didn't know. Maureen and Tim were pretty close. She wanted to meet me. Katie lived about ninety minutes from my house. We decided to meet somewhere in between. A date was set. That was the first time I talked to a sibling. I had a good friend growing up who I always considered a sibling. It was Steve, and he was the best man in my wedding. It was another irony. I had been a Steve for the first eight weeks of my life. There were so many ironies.

ABOUT THE BROOKSHIERS

I had found Maureen; now it was time to find out about Don. Maureen didn't have anything good to say about Don. She looked for his picture, but based on our visit I could tell she was glad he died. I appreciated everything Maureen told me, but she was a scorned woman as far as he was concerned. Her view was bitter. I needed to find out more. Who was he? What was he like? What was his life about? Call it shallow, but I was interested in the male side of my genealogy. Maureen had indicated he was good looking, but that was it for his positive attributes. My visit led me to believe Maureen was a good, decent woman. But who really was Don? If he was as truly as awful as she described, why would she have gotten involved enough to bear a child? She simply said she was foolish.

Finding Don became an obsession. But wasn't that my norm? Everything about this whole ordeal had become an obsession. The junky needed another fix. I found Maureen, but that wasn't enough. I needed to find Don. The SSDI told me his social security number originated in Missouri. But based on my adoption file, his family was from Illinois. Was the adoption file wrong? Was Maureen wrong? Or was the federal government wrong? I decided to follow the path of the federal government. His social security file was registered in Milan, Missouri. I was a Wisconsin boy. Were my roots in Missouri?

It took me back to a friend from high school, Jeff Howe, whose family was from Missouri. Jeff befriended me as a result of Boy Scouts. He was very patient with my impatience. By the time I met Jeff, I was a social misfit who was fidgety and always seemed to be distracted by something. In the beginning of first grade, I was a straight A student. But according to my aunt, my mother tried to tell me that I was adopted around the age of six, but I didn't want to hear it. My grades dropped to the C and D range in the middle of first grade. Never did my grades again rise to my potential throughout my primary and secondary education years. Perhaps I blocked it out. Chic didn't pursue it, and Nic was grateful. A new reality was formed. Chic had always been straightforward, in a rather cruel sort of way to Nic. But for some reason, she chose to harbor his secret. Chic loved Nic. It was a relentless love. Following Nic's and Chic's advice, I picked the University of Wisconsin–Stout, three hundred miles away. Higher ACT scores compensated for the lower cumulative grade point average. I had a straight-A average, a 4.0, when I moved from Wauwatosa. Home was a place that harbored many secrets. Finally, I was away from home.

Yes, Don was from Missouri, and apparently so were my roots. Don's path was hard to follow. Maureen told her caseworker through the adoption process that he was from Illinois. Sylvia and I met in Illinois. If only I was from Illinois, maybe it would help spark a romantic flame in my marriage. But even the adoption gods seemed to be against me at this point. The more I searched, the more it seemed he was from northern

Missouri. Endless internet searches revealed nothing. In northern Missouri, Brookshier was a common name. I resulted to the old-fashioned mode of the telephone, and at last I finally had success. I called countless numbers of Brookshiers, and even Brookshires. Finally I called a man who was a distant cousin to Don. When calling, I explained I was looking for a Brookshier whose father had died at an early age from a gunshot wound during the late 1930s. Maureen confirmed the story of Don's father was true. The cousin sounded like he was a surly sort of a fellow, but eager to help. He thought it was suicide, but nobody really knew. What? My grandfather committed suicide? I didn't probe further. All I needed as an emotional junky was another fix and a new lead. He was able to provide the name and number of Ina Peterson, Don's aunt. My groundwork was starting to pay off.

When I contacted Ina, she was very receptive. One of Don's paternal aunts, she was his father's sister. She was eager to talk. She missed her brother and wondered what happened to Don. While she wasn't thrilled with the prospect of having a bastard child in the family, she welcomed me with open arms. Who was I? Where was I from? Ina was full of just as many questions. She missed Don and was sad to hear he had died. It was her sister whom Don had spent time with during his youth while his mother worked. She recently had a hard time in dealing with her daughter's health issues. It caused her much pain, but that didn't seem to matter. Ina was a happy and grateful soul. As we talked, Ina disclosed Don's mother's name was Edna Owens before she married. She also told me of Don's other two sons, John and Guy. When Sally, her sister, died, she left John and Guy an inheritance. It was from the sale of Don's grandfather's family farm. I had more brothers. I couldn't believe it. Just three months ago, I was an only child. Now I had three brothers and one sister, not including the one who died early. I knew they were actually half siblings, but that really didn't matter. They were biological issue of my parents. "Issue" was a term I learned during my investigation of Scottish heritage. "Issue" was a term that described the offspring, whether it was legitimate or not. I was issue. My siblings were issue. We were common issue. Ina didn't have

John and Guy's phone number, but she had a number for Regina Sexton, their mother and Don's ex-wife.

I asked Ina if I could come to Iowa and visit her. Ina welcomed the thought of us visiting her. We were family. Christmas was rapidly approaching, and we decided it would be best to wait until the springtime, when travel was easier. In the meantime, we agreed to exchange pictures. I had a number of photos ready to go from the packet I sent to Margaret. It took Ina a little longer to locate her photos. About one week after I sent my packet to her, I received hers in the mail. It was the first picture I saw of my biological father. I guess our eyes were similar. It was a picture of him in high school, which I assumed to be a graduation picture. There was a wide assortment of pictures. which included earlier pictures of her and her sisters, pictures of her children at various ages, and even some of her grandchildren. For the first time I became aware of what the Brookshier side of my roots looked like. She had received my packet of photos before she was able to send hers. The photo she sent of her grandson had a striking resemblance to my son, Tony. When I called her, she indicated she also thought the two looked very familiar.

Additionally, Ina gave me the name and address of Glenna Brook. Glenna contacted Ina years earlier regarding the Brookshier family history, as she was compiling a thorough family history. Ina thought she might have more information. I called Glenna. She was a wealth of information. Glenna told me the Brookshiers and Brookhires had a common genealogy. Glenna quickly identified that she and I were connected only a few generations earlier in the family tree. She described the arrival of the Brookshiers in the mid-1600s, in Maryland. As far as ethnic heritage, Glenna indicated the original Brookshier's were English. She indicated, however, that over the last 250 years, and many generations since their arrival, the bloodline had seen a wide mix of various ethnic origins introduced. She thought this might have also included some Native American blood. She had a lot of documentation as a result of her genealogy work and would be willing to send me her book. At the time I didn't understand—the book was a complete and thorough history of the Brookshier family.

It was a Saturday afternoon, and I decided to take a chance. I checked directory assistance for the greater Toledo area. Once again I lucked out. Guy was listed. Sylvia was out with the kids. My heart was racing. I dialed. He answered. At first he didn't believe me. But then it seemed the amount of information I had gathered about Don convinced him there could be some validity to the story. As I listened to him talk, I noticed something strange. His accent was different, but something about the tone and pitch sounded familiar. It dawned on me. His voice sounded similar to my voice mail message at school. Our voices were similar.

Guy indicated he really had no conscious memory of Don. His mother left with him and John before he remembered much of anything. The only father he knew was Regina's second husband. Guy was a work-and-play-hard kind of person. He worked at the same grocery store chain since he had been in high school, where he eventually earned his way up to a management position. He had one daughter and was trying to work things out with her mother. John lived in Arizona, and Guy indicated they didn't have much contact. He hadn't seen him in a couple of years, but he told me he would try to get me John's phone number. I asked him if he thought it would be all right to contact Regina. He didn't see why not. If he couldn't find John's number, he knew she would have it.

THE BASTARD BEFORE YOU

The next call was a hard one. How would I approach an ex-wife of my biological father and possibly expose transgressions in his life? I had already assumed, since she was an ex-wife, there was most likely some strain in the relationship. The other peculiar thing was she lived in Ohio, just outside Toledo. Don's SSDI file indicated the place of his death was in Des Plains, Illinois. Now I had a new path leading me to Ohio. Undoubtedly, there were many more chapters of his life to unfold. Ina also indicated that, from what she remembered, Regina had left Don when the boys were very young.

Regina also seemed to have bitter memories of Don but was very kind and sympathetic to my situation. She did not know of my existence. Regina noted Don was a paratrooper and a Golden Gloves boxer in the air force. Regina was very young when they married, and within a year she was pregnant with John. She informed me that she was Don's second marriage. Regina thought Don's first wife's name might have been Mary. She believed Mary came with quite a bit of money and bought Don a bar to manage in the downtown loop of Chicago. Don enjoyed drinking, which eventually led to his demise in the bar business. Mary eventually got Don involved in her business, a beauty salon. It was close to O'Hare International Airport and serviced many of the flight attendants who flew in and out of Chicago. That's where she met Don. He was her beautician. She recalled that Mary was older than Don and may have had children from a previous marriage. He did not seem to be involved in Mary's children's lives. Regina believed Mary was ill and may have died. She believed Don was divorced from Mary prior to her death.

In addition to his drinking problem, Don had an explosive, jealous temper. He would often get physical with her. She recalled the first time was shortly after John was born. She decided to leave Don when John was only one or two. But one foolish slip resulted in her second pregnancy with Guy. She decided to tough it out a while longer. But by the time Guy was born, she knew she needed to leave. She decided to return to Ohio to be close to her family. Her family never liked Don; they just didn't trust him. Regina thought it was something about the way he looked. She left with the children, without letting Don know where they were going. She was afraid of Don's reaction. Only years later did she contact Don, via her lawyer, to initiate the divorce process. She wasn't aware of his death. She didn't think John or Guy knew either. I indicated I had talked with Guy. His father's death didn't seem to be an issue. She thought this was typical of Guy, just as it would have been with Don.

As we talked further, I asked if she had saved any pictures of Don. She thought she might have a few pictures of Don, and she even had some from his family. Regina confirmed that Edna Owens was his mother.

Regina had talked to Edna periodically, and thought she was an interesting woman. Edna loved Don very much. A nurse by trade later in life, her earlier years were spent singing on radio shows. Regina recalled Edna's family was in radio in the 1930s and 1940s somewhere around Texas. The name Tex Owens was one she remembered Edna talking about; she thought it was her brother. She recalled Tex was associated with the Grand Ole Opry. She mentioned that was why Don ended up being raised by his paternal grandparents and other relatives, as Edna was always on the road during Don's youth. Edna couldn't raise him and tend to the needs of her career at the same time. She needed the money. His grandparents loved Don, but Regina confirmed that Don's grandfather, Guy Brookshier, who Guy Junior was named after, was hard on Don. Regina thought she might have a picture of Edna. She also said she would send pictures of John and Guy. I told her I would send pictures to her of myself and my children, and would I appreciate her comments about any common physical features between Don and my family. She agreed.

Regina gave me John's phone numbers. She thought I would find it interesting talking to him, but cautioned the boys really never knew Don. Guy was a newborn when she left, and John couldn't have been older that two or three. Regina described John as being very much like herself, whereas Guy was a little Don. She had remarried and had another boy with her second husband. The boys all seemed to get along, but because of the differences in their personalities, they were somewhat distant. I asked her if she was familiar with what happened to Don after they parted. She indicated the last time she saw him was the night before she left with the boys. Regina indicated that Don had a half brother and two half sisters. Maybe they knew more. After Edna's first marriage to Don's father, Regina recalled Edna married two or three more times. She gave birth to Don's two sisters, Pat and Lee, through a man with the last name Hyatt. She thought Ron, the younger brother, was fathered by a man named Boyd Bracken. I thanked her, and she said I could call again if I had more questions. She also indicated she would be interested in hearing what else I discovered. She seemed to be a very gracious lady.

GETTING THE BRASS RING
(December 2000)

The last three months had been one of the most tumultuous periods in my life. I couldn't believe everything had changed so much. Just like a new parent learns to understand the longevity of parenting, I realized my change of circumstances was also permanent. This wasn't something I would just get used to. I was learning a new way to view my life and starting to understand much more about myself. The more I read about the characteristics of adoptees, the more I realized many of my actions, beliefs, and emotions were controlled by something I knew nothing about. But now the pace of the change turned from the fury of white water rapids to that of a deep, slow, winding river. I saw myself turn more inward; most of the time I was preoccupied. I recognized an anger and impatience had crept into many aspects of my life. I was sleeping and exercising less, and I was drinking more. The flow of information started to slow. Time began to move at a snail's pace.

I had started to mass quite a bit of information about Don, yet there were still large gaps. Maureen knew little. Ina had been helpful, and I thought if I could make a trip to see her, I would have more time to absorb what she knew. Regina told me a lot about Don's thirties, and early forties, but it looked like he died at the age of sixty. What happened to him after Regina left? Were there additional siblings? I just didn't know. I wanted to know. I needed to know. I contacted De Page County, where Don died, and ordered a copy of his death certificate. Maybe it would shed more clues. I wondered who signed Don's death certificate. He could have married again, and if so, maybe it would lead me to more siblings. Besides, there was something concrete about holding someone's death certificate—something more personal. I also conducted an SSDI search for Edna Owens. She had died in May 2000, just five months before my discovery. I was frustrated by the fact I missed her by so little time. But once again I had more clues to follow.

A long-awaited day finally arrived. I received the copy of my original birth certificate in the mail. Once Maureen agreed to release my identity, I was allowed to receive it. The date, time, and attending physician remained the same. Everything else had been fabricated to support the lie. In a way, I thought this was the equivalent of legalized perjury, committed by the state. What would be my sentence if I committed the same crime? While I realized, this is the dream of every adoptee, I knew my hunger wasn't satisfied. I still needed more. I met Maureen, I found out some pieces of information about Don, and I even had talked to siblings. Why wasn't I satisfied? I just didn't understand. All I knew was I had to keep on the trail. Like a dog pursuing the scent of a rabbit, I found myself compelled to keep my nose to the ground, as I ran through endless acres of thickets. Unaware of my surroundings, my only focus was that what I was hunting.

As the autumn faded into winter, the weather started to change at an accelerated pace. I had always loved winter. There was a crispness in the air that had a cleansing effect on the soul. Nighttime eventually dominated each twenty-four-hour period. Darkness was the rule of the land. But I realized once the cold, hard grip of winter had blown into its full furry, beach walks would become impossible. I had relied on those walks to process what was happening. I felt a connection to something when I walked the sandy beach alone. Was it an ancestor from my past, was it the spirit of my mother Chic, or was it simply me getting in touch with a side that had been held hostage by a secret for forty-one years? I wasn't sure what it was, but I knew I needed it. I was lucky. As the solstice neared, winter had been slow in coming, but Christmas was rapidly approaching. It didn't feel like Christmas. I was getting depressed. Sylvia's mother came to visit from Pennsylvania. It was a time for family, but I didn't feel like I really had any family. We received the onslaught of salutary Christmas cards and even managed to send our own. Ours was a family picture taken shortly before my discovery. It seemed like it had been taken many lifetimes ago. I knew I loved my children, and I thought I must love my wife, but I didn't feel love. I didn't feel much of anything except bouts of anger. I frequently thought of my father's death. But nothing really felt like family. Like a broken wineglass, all I saw were fragments of what had once been a complete life. The glass wasn't half full; it wasn't even half empty. It was shattered and completely empty.

As I took the last walk of the year on New Year's Eve, I thought back to the previous New Year's, when a recently divorced friend, Dean, and his two children joined us to celebrate the new millennium. I half-heartedly joked, "If we made it through the eighties, then the nineties, what were we in now? The oh-ohs." If only I knew.

At last the holidays were behind me. I hadn't been shy about talking to anyone who would be willing to listen to my saga. I always put on a happy face and treated it like a great adventure. My uncle Bob once told me that I always managed to see the silver lining in every cloud. I always made it look that way, at least. But following every adventurous story time came a darker, more inward time. I was even surprised at myself. I hated what happened. How could I be so fucking joyous about it? I no longer trusted my adoptive family. I still harbored too much anger to go down that road. All I had from my birth family was bits and pieces, along with pictures of people I didn't even know. Most of the few I met, I had known for less than a month or two. My birth mother allowed me to find out who I was, but only at the expense of never divulging her identity. I knew it was all I asked for, but it was like Pandora's box. I needed to be acknowledged.

A COMFORTABLE DIVERSION

Dean joined us again during the Presidents' Day weekend. It was late winter in 2001. As we were sitting around reading the Sunday paper before Dean took his children back to his ex-wife, I made an offhand comment to Sylvia regarding an ad I saw about two snowmobiles with a trailer for sale. I always wanted snowmobiles, and even thought they could be a great family activity for us all to have to enjoy the long Wisconsin winters. Sylvia had always been against the idea, indicating it was too dangerous. This time there were two snowmobiles, one for me and one for her. Now it seemed like a better idea. We went, looked, and bought. Even though neither of us had driven snowmobiles before, we both thought a fresh beginning of a new activity might be a welcomed relief. I was hoping I was snapping back to my old adventurous self, someone who was able to go out and explore new beginnings, not just research an old abandoned past. I spent endless hours carting the kids around our two-acre lot. I think it was my old friend denial creeping back into my life. While we enjoyed the snowmobiles for the few remaining days of winter, it wasn't long before they needed to be parked, and the junky needed another fix.

One very good friend of mine, Sam, was married to a woman who was a birth mother; she had given up a baby when she was young. I wasn't aware of this until I spilled my guts. It turned out Ellen, my friend's wife, had been going through the reverse process. Her surrendered son had recently turned eighteen. She wanted to know what happened to him. She was as driven as I was. As we talked, she confessed, she knew who he was, and where he lived. At first I didn't think it was possible. I had played the adoption identity game, and knew the process. She didn't go through the state, how could she find him? It turned out it was simpler than I thought. Birth records are public information. She knew the date and time he was born. All she had to do was go to the county of his birth, Milwaukee, and search for the right time of birth, on the day he was born. She had first found him while he was in his early teens, but opted not to contact him until he was eighteen, as she didn't want to disrupt his upbringing. She lucked out; he was born and adopted in the same county, the same as me.

It turned out the only one in this game with no recourse is the one who had nothing to do with it, the orphan. As an orphan, I simply needed to be grateful for the gift of life, which I am. But life is comprised of more than biological facts and medical information. I realized it also has something to do with the human experience; to know whom oneself is, to have dignity. I felt a whole new level of understanding of what discrimination was about. I was part of a class of people denied rights to something the rest of the population enjoyed.

I decided perhaps that's why abortion was so prevalent. It's easier to deal with a simple flush, than work through a lifetime of relationships. I still believed in choice versus state control, but I thought the privilege comes with understanding. Once again I related to the Bastard Nation. It seemed funny. I was born of bitterness, and like a disease, it spread. As time unfolded, Ellen and I became good friends, and shared each side of our paths with each other. It provided balance to a potentially explosive situation. It probably saved me in the long run from being sucked into a perpetual vortex of anger so familiar to many adoptees.

Eventually, I was able to contact John Brookshier. A couple of months had slipped by since I first found out about him. He turned out to be fairly elusive, and kind of a free spirit. He had been living outside Phoenix and was working at a Kinko's. He didn't care for the cold Toledo winters and was enjoying winter in the warm desert sun. As we talked, I recognized a trait we shared. Our conversation seemed to take on a life of its own. While some people follow a logical sequence to their thoughts in conversation, others allow for a much more random approach. While it can be frustrating to some, it was comforting to me. Additionally, John, by his own confession, had a specific health-related issue. Between his free spirit and his health-related issue, he was an individual with a dislike for education. One of my children had the same health-related issue. I wasn't surprised to find it in the family tree. John didn't remember much about Don, but he did remember more than Guy. That wasn't really a surprise. He was more interested in Don and his family than Guy. He seemed to be sad to hear of Don's death.

Around this time, Sylvia noted I was changing. While I was aware of the change, I couldn't pinpoint what it was. It started to affect every aspect of my life. It was anger. Unfortunately, anger permeates everything in one's life. Like cancer, it's a tumor that will eventually, if left undiscovered, spread to everything that is you. I had begun to metastasize. The cancer had spread. It's obvious *to others*, but not to the victim. I didn't realize the extent that it was affecting my life.

LOOK, MA. I'M FAMOUS.
(FEBRURARY 2001)

In late February, a reporter from the *Ozaukee Press* contacted me. Carol, the reporter, said she had talked to Ellen about the other side of adoption and became interested in my story. Would I be willing to be interviewed for an article for the *Ozaukee Press*? To me, my story was incomplete. Why would it be interesting? She indicated it was a great human-interest story, and it would make good press. I told her I would need to think about it. After all, I was a teacher in the community, and I needed to think about how it would affect my family and my students. But as I thought about it, I realized people needed to understand my frustration. Here I was a successful, forty-one year old adult, who kept his p's and q's in order, and suddenly I was thrust into a different world—a punitive world with many restrictions. Maybe my story would help people understand the futility I felt I was going through. To me, it was self-evident, but others didn't seem to have a clue. While everyone else was enjoying the professed freedom from living in the United States, I felt like I was living in the stifling government secrecy of Cold War Russia. The problem was my address was Small Town, Wisconsin, but my new reality was Communist Moscow. I agreed to do the article.

Carol did a good job. It seemed to summarize where I was at in the process and yet gave a personal touch to my story. She showed pictures of me and my family, along with pictures of Don and his family. Yet I found little response. Sure, there were the acknowledgments of "Fred, I read your story." And even an occasional, "I had no idea." Some in my small community saw me more as an embarrassment, versus something to embrace. But no one seemed to understand the profound effect it was having on me. I was changing as the result of the loss of my old foundation. As anger and mistrust replaced optimism and compassion, I found I had obstacles and limited access to the information I needed to help myself. Information about my past, and where I had come from was what I needed to build a new foundation. Man-made legal constraints blocked my ability to do so.

MORE ABOUT THE BROOKSHIERS

In the meantime, Glenna's book of the Brookshier family tree arrived. It was thick. At first I only glanced through it. I realized the Brookshier family had dated back to the late 1600s in North America, but I really didn't understand the intricacies of the family tree. Once again I called Glenna. She quickly led me through the generations to identify on which pages, of which there were over three hundred, my ancestors were located. The book also came complete with pictures. Some of the pictures dated back to the Civil War, one of which was my great-great-great-grandfather, William Jasper Brookshier. It was the first time I realized, despite the actions of William's offspring, my relationship with him was no different than anyone else's with their more distant ancestors. The thought occurred to me: Would I not also welcome back my great-great-great-grandson, even if his subsequent father had allowed for his adoption? I felt a spiritual connection to William.

CHAPTER 3

MEETING THE RELATIVES

DON'S AUNT INA
(MARCH 2001)

In March 2001, it had been six months since my initial discovery. It was time to contact Ina and arrange the visit. Spring break was approaching, and it would be a perfect time to make a trip to northern Iowa. The call was made, and arrangements were underway. Sylvia and I decided to make it a brief spring break family vacation to Iowa. It wasn't that far away, and the kids might enjoy staying in a hotel with a pool. Ina was excited for my family to come to visit. She decided it would be a sort of family reunion, and she would have her children and grandchildren come to meet us.

We arrived at midday, around three, checked into the room, and unloaded our suitcases from the van. The kids were anxious to go swimming, but I wanted to touch base with Ina before it got too late. When I called, she was anxious for us to come over. Some of her family were able to make it later that evening, but some had other commitments. We agreed to let the kids go swimming to burn off some of the energy from being pent up in the van much of the day.

We arrived at her house around five. The sun was fading, but there was still plenty of light for the kids to play outside her house for a while. It was a nice tree-lined neighborhood in Cedar Rapids, Iowa. It felt peaceful. Ina must have been in her late seventies or eighties, but she seemed very sharp and physically capable. She had mentioned she owned some rental properties and still did some of the maintenance herself. Everything about the setting seemed to fit what I would have imagined Cedar Rapids to be like. I hadn't really spent any time in Iowa before. My great-aunt Ina seemed really nice.

She brought us into her home, and we all went through the introductions. Ina suggested my kids and her grandkids play outside while the grown-ups got to know each other. There was a small park across the street, and my kids were eager to be with the other kids. Tony mentioned, "Her house smelled funny." I met her grandson, who looked like my youngest. The similarity was striking, although Mike, Ina's grandson, was older than I would have imagined. Ina indicated she had purposefully sent a picture of him when he was Tony's age to highlight the similarity in the boy's appearance. Initially, everyone was curious to hear about my ordeal. But before I knew it, we were talking about the weather, hunting, and trucks. It felt very Iowa and very welcoming. As we prepared to head back to the hotel, everyone thanked us for coming and wished us a safe ride back. I said I would return alone tomorrow to go through family pictures and other information Ina had. It felt like a family gathering.

The next morning I returned. Sylvia agreed to take the kids to see the sights of Cedar Rapids. To this day, I still have no idea what exactly they did. Ina had several boxes of pictures, articles, and various other artifacts. While I had already seen a few pictures of Don as an adult, Ina had many from Don's youth. There were pictures taken at Don's grandfather's farm.

Ina also had several pictures of Edna at various ages as well as some of Don's father, my grandfather.

As Ina talked about Don, I could see her travel back to the time of Don's youth. He was very athletic, but he struggled with academics. When he lived with Edna, he was transferred to many different schools, as she moved frequently. Eventually, he went to live with his grandparents, and his school life stabilized for the remainder of his high school days. She remembered he was a lively boy, but he was always kind and polite. He seemed to be responsible, so my sudden appearance was quite a shock. She hadn't heard from him, or about his whereabouts, since around the time I was born. I found that interesting. She knew when her father died he tried to find Don but couldn't. That brought him sadness during his final days.

I asked Ina about the cousin who indicated Don's father, her brother, committed suicide. She adamantly denied it. Ina was in the house at the time. She said there was a squirrel in the bathroom, and Don Sr. slipped with a loaded gun, which discharged and killed him. It was a great tragedy. I further probed about Don's parents' divorce. She thought the reason Edna left her brother was on account of her desire for a singing career. Don's father wanted to stay on the family farm, whereas Edna was a beautiful, talented, and ambitious woman who found rural farm life too slow. Ina didn't think they had been married for more than two years before Edna left. She wasn't certain they ever really divorced. Edna may have been a widow at a very young age.

It was getting later in the morning when I asked Ina if I could take materials to a nearby Kinko's to make color photos. She agreed. By early afternoon I had completed my mission, rounded up Sylvia and the kids, and returned to Ina's. We made our final farewells. It was a sad departure. Even though I had spent so little time with my great-aunt Ina, I already knew I would miss her. She had provided so much information, shown me so many pictures into my biological past, and provided insight into not just what people looked like but who they were.

As we drove off, I realized I had come to know a new side of me. I knew my family had raised me as a Nicora, but now I felt a connection to the Brookshiers. I was no longer only of Romanian-Polish heritage but also one of English-Irish and Norwegian-German heritage. While it may seem insignificant, to me it meant the world of difference. It's not that my old heritage was less but it did offer a different on my perspective of who I was. As Americans, we value what we do, not who we are. Or do we? How much money has been spent on family genealogy? How much has been spent on documenting exactly when we came here, and who fought in what war? As an orphan, all those pieces of the genealogical past become inaccessible. Adopted people have no way of finding out the answers to any of those questions. It seemed it was similar to grafting a cherry tree to the roots of an apple tree. Society's assumptions were now the tree would produce apples. But they don't. I didn't mind bearing cherries; I just needed to understand why. I further asked, *Is that what our ancestors, who risked their lives to defend a future for their families, would have wanted?* I think not. I was issue. I mattered.

ADJUSTMENTS AND AFTERSHOCKS

When we made it back to Wisconsin, I realized I had found out so much from my visit to Iowa. I came back with an array of photos and documentation of who I was. I had hit a mother lode. Everything I found was authentic. Ina had the equivalent of a pot of gold at the end of a rainbow. I now had photos, descriptions, and even original documentation of new aspects of who I was. Satisfaction was on the horizon. I decided to put together a photo album. I had pictures of my mother's side of the family as well as those of my father's. The two sides couldn't exist on the same page, but it could still be my own personnel family photo album. I could always add to it as I found more. But for now, it would serve as my documentation of my new, expanded life.

Sylvia had been with me though everything, yet she still was struggling with how I was dealing with it all. As I had lost myself, she was also losing herself. With three kids under the age of eight, it seemed insanity was only one step away. Yet the baggage continued to disguise the truth. I had become more distant and preoccupied. She could see I was slipping away. She needed help. She could see I needed help. She suggested I find a counselor to talk to. It wasn't the first time she suggested I see a counselor. On the other hand, after ten years of marriage, I thought she also needed a counselor.

Several years ago, when we lived in Minneapolis, she thought our marriage needed help. At the time my mother was dying, and I felt out of control. But to me it didn't seem like I could afford to squeeze another minute into my schedule. The thought of taking the time to haggle over unimportant issues was incomprehensible. After all, my mother was dying. That's what mattered. I was making weekly trips to Milwaukee as I was trying to hold my life and teaching career together. Just when I probably needed it the most was the time I was the most unlikely to be receptive to it. Only later did I realize my harbored secret was blinding me. At the time I wasn't consciously aware that I was living under a lie. Whereas having a professional help me see my motives and behaviors would have been the most sensible thing to do, a deeper, inner side of me did not, could not, face my deepest motives. Denial was so much easier than facing reality. I had no way to know I was simply trying to avoid an inner truth. The inner truth that somewhere deep inside me was a truth I couldn't bare to face. I wasn't yet ready to hear what I needed to hear.

In a way, it seemed marriage was the pairing of two people who were willing to cover each other's secrets. The lives we can't bare to face are an agreement we decide to harbor. If mine hadn't been revealed yet, what was the point of going to counseling? In many ways, I was right. But in other ways, I was fatally wrong. What I didn't realize at the time was my concealed secret—my adoption that even I wasn't consciously aware of— wasn't our entire problem. And maybe had I made time for counseling we could have avoided our final fate. But I didn't.

This time my secret was out in the open, even to me. Suddenly the thought of seeing a counselor seemed appropriate. I willingly agreed and made an appointment with a counselor in Sheboygan. I had gotten his name through my school's employee assistance program. When I met with him, I was surprised to see how much younger he was than I. After all, my entire life I had come to believe counselors were supposed to come with gray beards. This one didn't even have a gray hair on his head. Here I was, having shaved the few gray hairs on my head years ago, talking to a person who supposedly would know more about my situation than I did. It was my first experience with a counselor, and I didn't realize that just because he was younger than I was didn't necessarily mean I knew more about his studied profession than he did. But I came armed with photo album in hand. I felt my assembled photo album of my acquired family would be enough to get me through the litmus test. At this point I was still only visiting the counselor to appease a marital discrepancy.

As we talked, he seemed to ask a variety of questions that dealt with broad issues. How did I feel about the adoption? How was I sleeping? Did I have any suicidal thoughts? Did I have a full range of emotions? Why did I come here? After he looked at my adoption photo album, he indicated I seemed to be dealing with it as well as anyone given my situation would. I was happy to give Sylvia my report card. In retrospect, I think I was as honest as I could have been.

The school year was coming to an end, and I had received Don's death certificate. It was signed by Ron Bracken. He was Don's half brother from a later marriage of Edna's. I thought if I could find Ron Bracken maybe I could find out what happened to Don the second half of his life, once he went off the radar screen from the rest of his family. Regina indicated Ron went to law school in Colorado. Edna had told Regina he always wanted to be a lawyer. I searched the internet for Ron Backen in Colorado. Nothing surfaced. Regina mentioned Edna lived in Florida for a while, so I thought maybe Ron could be found there. I tried Florida and once again found nothing. I decided to broaden my search. There were hundreds of Ron Brackens. I started to resort to blind phone calls to see if any of the Ron Brackens were the one I was looking for. Again I found nothing. Elusiveness ran in the family. Just like John Brookshier, Ron was an abstract character. Once again, like the dog in the thicket, my nose was to the ground, and my hunt was on. But the more I searched, the more I found Ron was a dead end. I couldn't find him or the answers to what happened to Don the last twenty years of his life.

I also started to explore Tex Owens. I was hopeful that if he had been somewhat famous, as Regina had indicated, maybe there would be something about him on the internet. Furthermore, perhaps something about him might lead to more information about Edna, and even possibly to Ron Bracken. I was right about my first assumption. Tex's name was a hit. There were many listings, most of which tied him to the Grand Ole Opry Hall of Fame. He apparently wrote many songs and recorded several. There was also a *Best of Tex Owens* CD available through Amazon. I placed an order and received it several days later. Unfortunately, my second assumption didn't pan out. There wasn't any mention of Edna or Ron.

My reliance on the late-discovery adoptee group had grown. I had found people I could relate to. They were the only ones in this insanity who really seemed to understand what I was going through. The postings on the website seemed to correlate to each and every one of my feelings. While teaching school, I often would seek the words of comfort from those I could most closely associate with. As I hung on to my daily ritual of my family and career, I would seek comfort from the postings of those I had found. They were the ones who were also searching for answers. More often than not, they were bitter from the lack of access to information. Day after day was full of postings on the website seeking answers to questions that could be found, but they were the only ones who couldn't receive the answers because of legal constraints. I had already found so many answers, but for me there were still so many questions unanswered. Most of the participants were still stuck in the legal entanglement of finding out who their mothers were. Some states, and most other developed countries, offer an open record status. That means once an adoptee turns eighteen they have free access to their birth records. It's really a much simpler, less costly system. There are no social workers acting as intermediaries. The adoptee simply has free, open access to find out about who they are. It eliminates governmental involvement. Birth records are simply birth records. There is no shame; there is no embarrassment on either side. The beautiful birth of a child is simply that—nothing else.

Sylvia and I were becoming more distant by the day. She had taken a teaching position in Sheboygan. To her, the job was a refuge from the isolation on the lake, the kids, and me. The year at home was hard. Sylvia valued her professional life. The year without that outlet had taken its toll; teaching high school was a deeply entrenched part of her personality. At last she was able to engage with who she really was. While the first year of a teaching job is a demanding job, she found comfort in meeting and interacting with new adult colleagues.

Sylvia's time alone with Tony was that of isolation. During that first year, following the move, I was either at school or preparing for school at home. I also kept my weight-lifting routine going by using the weight room at the high school. That meant I was gone from in the morning until six in the evening. Typically, Sylvia's day was spent getting the girls ready for the school bus to pick them up, tending to Tony's every want and need, cleaning the house from the previous day, cooking, and then hunkering down for the firestorm that would start to arrive. Madeline attended morning kindergarten and would arrive back home on the bus around noon. Grace would typically come back from first grade around three. To Sylvia, from the time Grace walked in the door until the kids were put into bed around eight, the hurricane seemed like a category five. While Sylvia loved the house and living on the lake, there were no other adults to talk to. The summer was approaching, and she knew it would mean back to being trapped in the house.

What was it about the house that Sylvia loved? It was a beautiful house in a beautiful setting. Initially, it was the fact she lived on the lake. When we moved there, we were referred to as lake bitches. Many wanted and sought after a Lake Michigan address. What most didn't realize was it came with a stigma. It meant you weren't anybody to associate with. We made some friends, but overall we found the community rather cold. We came to love our neighbors and those who accepted us. The house itself also had issues. It was designed in the early 1990s by a self-owner architect who was a staunch believer in the postmodern philosophy. Specifically, it was a contemporary home with references to the past. It was actually a six-level split-open concept. That translated to too many levels with few doors and few barriers. Every level was connected. It was a nightmare to anyone trying to raise young children. The advantage was we could hear the kids' every move. The disadvantage was we could hear the kids' every move. There was no privacy. There was no separate life for the adults living in the house. We were a family—all the time. During that first year, Sylvia had no escape. She was home all the time, every day.

My feelings about the house were very different. While I loved aspects of the house, it also turned out to be a maintenance nightmare. Yes, it was beautiful, but she required too much to maintain. Because of the ten-foot ceilings and the six stories, it was very tall. Caulk and paint required thirty-foot ladders. Living on Lake Michigan fulfilled many dreams. At the same time, though, it also brought as many issues. The Lake Michigan ecosystem was harsh. It realizes extreme temperature changes with high variations in humidity. Anybody with natural wood siding and a water-based stain needed to paint every three years just to keep ahead of the pealing. With three kids and a teaching job, there was no way I could keep up with the maintenance. Eventually, I came to hate the house that fulfilled many of my dreams. I couldn't keep up with it while trying to find a new identity. Before my discovery it seemed within reason. My available time was drained by the search.

Our other problem was our apartment building. After we settled into the community, we decided to buy a rental property with the money my parents left me. It seemed like a good investment, as I didn't want to squander the inheritance. I had paid off bills, bought a few toys for my family and myself, but I felt the rest should work for their grandchildren. To this day, I still feel like that was a good strategy. But the apartment building was already starting to take its toll. Before my discovery it seemed like there was plenty of time to take care of all my needs and deal with the needs of a small apartment building. But as my search sucked away time from my family, it also sucked away the available time to tend to the needs of tenants and the building. I managed to keep my job throughout the ordeal. My own personal interests suffered, however. While the first two years of ownership went without a hitch, my distractions resulted in disgruntled tenants and empty apartments. Specifically, before my discovery, I spent much more time helping the tenants negotiate common grounds on which they could find a basis to live in a common building. After my discovery they were pretty much on their own. Soon it became evident it was time to sell the building. The requirements of being a landlord had begun to encroach on the remaining time I had for my family and my job. Something had to give. My search was taking a lot of time. The apartment building went on the market.

Both Sylvia and I were off for the summer, and the girls had started morning summer school, with the afternoons off. I had many projects to complete. The house was short on outside storage space. So I built two storage sheds over the course of the summer with the help of Ellen's husband. He was a salt-of-the-earth kind of guy. More than anything, he valued the ability to be self-sufficient and help his friends. Sam, Ellen's husband, seemed to like helping kindred spirits. He grew up on the lake, a few miles from our home, so he seemed to enjoy my association with the lake. Sam was a welder and could do just about anything on his own. That seemed to pretty much summarize the characteristics of the people around here. Self-sufficiency was a norm in the community. One of the significant lessons I learned from moving from a suburban lifestyle into this rural community was that in the city people figured out how to get things done. That often meant hiring the right people to do what they needed done and earning enough money to do so. In rural Wisconsin, people figured out how to do things. They didn't hire someone in a trade to do the work they needed completed; they simply figured out how to do the work themselves. It was an interesting lesson. On the flip side, it had an entirely new implication for my chosen profession. I had to teach these kids how to do all these things, not just teach them how to get them done. The latter would have been a much easier lesson.

Toward the end of summer, Sylvia took the kids out to Pennsylvania to visit her family. She was born and raised in Lancaster, Pennsylvania, but moved to Wisconsin to attend graduate school in Madison. Her first job following the completion of her degree was at SwedishAmerican Hospital (Swed's) in Rockford, Illinois, in the planning department. She was a staff planner, as she had earned a master's degree in public health administration. I also took a position in the planning department at Swed's. I had completed an undergraduate degree in business administration and was near completion of my graduate degree in management technology, pending completion of my thesis. Swed's was where we first met. After six months of working together, I moved to California to work as a consultant. Eventually, several years later, we both lived in Milwaukee, Wisconsin, where we attended the University of Wisconsin–Milwaukee (UWM). Sylvia was obtaining her teaching license, whereas I was earning a master of architecture degree. UWM was where we started dating and fell in love. After completing my degree, I accepted my first architectural position in Minneapolis, Minnesota. Sylvia followed, and within a year we married. But every year Sylvia made her annual pilgrimage back to Pennsylvania to visit her family. Some years I went with her, but this year I didn't. I had been working on many projects around the house, and we decided she would make the trip with the kids alone. To some extent, I think we each wanted a break from each other.

While the family was gone, in addition to tending to my work tasks around the house, I decided to pull one of our kayaks into Lake Michigan and watch the sunset from about three hundred yards into the lake. It was a particularly quiet evening on the lake; it was as smooth as glass. I had taken a couple of bottles of Guinness with me to help me enjoy the relaxing moment. As I floated in my solitude, I couldn't help but thinking about how this particular moment seemed to be a metaphor for my life at this point. I felt very alone and very adrift. I seemed to make a deep connection with myself as well as my surroundings during my float. At that moment I felt one with nature, one with my ancestors, and one with myself. It was very tranquil. Maybe it was the Guinness.

BROTHER TIM
(JULY 2001)

As the lush emerald greens of early summer matured into deeper and darker shades, I completed my projects, Sylvia managed to deal with the kids, and my search came to a stall. Many beach walks dominated my moonlit nights, yet not much progress was found on finding Don or what happened to him after I was born. I continued to talk to Maureen and Katie. Toward the end of summer, Maureen indicated Tim was ready to talk. He had been living just outside West Bend but had taken a job transfer to another state. He would be leaving soon and agreed to meet me before he left. I was elated. Finally, I would get to meet another sibling—Katie's brother and Maureen's other son. I called him, and we made arrangements. It was to be a lunch meeting at Applebee's in West Bend. I couldn't wait.

The day came, and I felt like the Hunchback of Notre Dame. At last I would be let out of the bell tower and into the public eye. What a joyous day it was. Just before I entered Applebee's, I looked over the parking lot to see if I could identify his car. I recalled Maureen mentioned he drove a Corvette. There one was. He must be here. But, no, wait—there was another. Which one is his? Maybe neither was his. I just didn't know. All I knew was he would be about five eight, with brown hair. We were to meet at the bar. It was approaching noon on an ideal summer day, so the bar was nearly empty. Was I wrong about the date or time? I didn't think so. But Tim didn't seem to be there. How many people own Corvettes? I was nervous.

Eventually, Tim entered. He looked similar to Maureen, so immediately I recognized him. As our lunch date progressed, our conversation went from awkward to relaxed. An intelligent engineer, Tim was direct and to the point. It became evident he had gotten over the difficulties of the situation and was ready to talk to me without pretense. We discussed what we had accomplished, what our goals and ambitions were, and a small amount about his surprise with my existence. Before I knew it we had finished eating, and it was time to make our pleasant goodbyes.

Overall, I viewed the meeting as a success. I'm not sure how he viewed the encounter. While I enjoyed and benefited from the meeting, I also realized he and Maureen had pretty much the same personality, which was different than mine. It's not that I minded, but it did leave me with the burning question: Where did my personality come from? My mind was drawn back to my search for Don. I still felt wanting.

BROTHERS JOHN AND GUY—TOLEDO
(August 2001)

As the colors of the season began to show the brilliance of another fall, I had gotten word John had returned to Toledo. It was the perfect opportunity to meet both John and Guy. Toledo was only about seven hours away, and I could easily make a trip there and back in a weekend. While Guy had been receptive in the beginning, he had grown more elusive. John, on the other hand, seemed more welcoming as time passed by. Regina continued to be interested in my findings and was always helpful during my phone calls with her. When I suggested I come out for a visit, Regina seemed to view it as having positive potential for her boys. She helped arrange lodging at a local motel and identified a place for our first meeting. She would coordinate the schedule between the boys and me. I was open to whatever she suggested.

The drive from southeastern Wisconsin to Toledo provided long hours of isolation, which was a perfect time to reflect. I had spoken with both John and Guy on the phone and had made initial impressions about what our similarities and differences were. After all, while we shared the same biological father, we came from different mothers. Additionally, as an educator, I had become well acquainted with the nature versus nurture debate. I couldn't say which side of the argument I really agreed with, but I did know I felt both were important. Why was I driven to go out to meet them? I knew I wasn't searching for any long-lost sibling relationship. I realized those relationships were a privilege to those who grew up in the same household—on the nurture side. Then what was I seeking? I certainly had invested too much into whatever I was looking for. As I drove, I decided it was more about finding a part of me. I was looking for a greater understanding in how I acted and where my inner drive came from. Both positive and negative traits of Nic and Chic were ingrained in my personality. I knew what they had contributed, but there were still voids. I decided that while the boys were great unknowns I needed to understand them. Maybe if I met my other siblings I could get a better understanding of the missing pieces within me. All I knew was I had to.

Once I arrived in Toledo, I found my motel and checked into my room. It was a Friday afternoon, and I was to call Regina around three. My understanding was Regina had some kind of an administrative job in a real estate firm. She had said once she received my call she would tell me where she, John, Guy, and I could meet for supper. When I called, it seemed like all was in order, and Regina indicated the restaurant was only a couple of blocks from my motel. Regina made reservations for 5:45 p.m. The plan was to meet at the restaurant.

I was anxious to finally meet my half brothers on Don's side. From my phone conversations, I had already detected that Guy seemed a little higher strung, while John seemed to be fairly laid back. Regina had sent pictures of them at various ages, so I had some notion of who I was looking for. Regina had also sent a picture of her and Don from their wedding. She looked to be a very attractive woman, with full dark hair and dark eyes. According to Regina, John really didn't look much like Don, except in his eyes. She indicated John's eyes had the overall structure of Don's, but John's eyes were brown like hers. Regina indicated Don had very intense blue eyes. She had described Guy to be just like Don, in both overall body structure and temperament. She also thought that, as far as appearance, Guy had a stronger resemblance to Don.

I arrived around five thirty and decided to make my way to the bar and have a drink. This was definitely a Scotch and water affair. I had a double. The drink flowed down like water, despite the fact its color was that of pure Scotch. Another quickly followed it. The bar was positioned to provide a good view of the entrance. It allowed me to scour each new arrival to see if any were my targets. I recognized Regina first, as she really hadn't changed much from her wedding picture. Like the picture of her walking down the aisle, she had shorter brown hair, with larger almond-shaped brown eyes. Her appearance was rather sultry, in a Mrs. Robinson sort of way. She was a beautiful woman. I then figured out she must be with John. To me, he didn't look much like what I imagined him to be. As I studied his features, I realized the most recent picture I had seen of him must be several years old. To me, he had a strong Brookshier look. I had recently seen many pictures of the Brookshiers during my visit to Ida's house in Iowa, and there was a commonality of features in the nose, jaw, and overall facial structure. But Regina seemed to be right. Outside the eye structure, he didn't seem to look much like what I imagined Don to look like. Although, despite the numerous pictures I had seen of Don, I still had a hard time tying the various pictures of Don into a single look. Despite feelings of anxiousness and hesitation, I found myself rising and proceeding to the entrance to see if I had picked the right people. Maybe it was the liquid courage. The restaurant was getting fairly busy at this point, and the vestibule was crowded with many strange faces.

"Hi, Regina?" I inquired.

"Oh, Fred. Yes, I see it in your eyes. You've got Don's eyes."

"Ah, thanks, I think," I awkwardly responded. "Thank you for meeting me."

I was surprised at her directness regarding my appearance so early in the conversation. I didn't know if there was a predictable path for the conversation, given the circumstances. I think we were both stumbling for the correct protocol. But her simple acknowledgment of my similar appearance to Don seemed to make me feel at ease and more comfortable about making the trip. It now seemed like I did the right thing.

"This is John," she continued. "Guy has a delay and should join us shortly."

As we moved beyond the introductory formalities, we made our way to our table. The restaurant seemed to have a barbeque theme, in a nicer sort of way. Both John and Regina seemed fairly relaxed and eager to get to know more about me. The conversation progressed into a pleasant exchange of information and gradually allowed for a level of personal sharing of feelings and emotions. John remained fairly quiet at first, but then seemed to settle in, as I perceived him to view me as less of a threat and more of a curiosity. It was the first time he ever had an older brother.

Just as we were about to order, Regina recognized Guy in the vestibule. She signaled him over and we went back to introductions. Guy explained he had been detained at work and needed to leave in a short while to see his daughter. He shared his daughter with a woman he had been dating for a while—years before they had moved in together, which was when she became pregnant. After his daughter was born, Debbie, his girlfriend, came to the conclusion their relationship wasn't working. Guy moved out. But he felt it important to remain part of his daughter's life. This included both a physical presence through weekly visits and outings as well as financial support. After a brief period, Guy said he needed to leave. While he couldn't stay long, I was able to get an overall sense of who he was. Guy seemed to be somewhat driven, very task oriented, and worked many hours at his job. We exchanged our farewells and agreed to keep in periodic contact.

Our meals arrived, and the conversation continued to cover a wide range of topics. Many of the topics centered on Don and what Regina knew about his life. John seemed just as interested as I was. It became apparent that his name didn't come up much as he grew up. Regina was interested in what Maureen was like. In particular, she wanted to know Maureen's zodiac sign. She was a believer of astrology and indicated "your father" also believed in the fate of the stars. I was relieved that Regina seemed relaxed about discussing Don. My experience with Maureen was not the same. While both women really didn't have many nice things to say about Don, Regina's demeanor was more relaxed and objective in its tone. Given she was married to him for a while, I thought that wasn't too surprising. From Maureen's perspective, she had basically been jilted before she even made it to the altar and forced to deal with cleaning up the mess by herself. The loss of control during an unwanted pregnancy seemed to have taken its toll. Regina, on the other hand, had spent several years with Don, and even bore a second child to him. It was Regina who finally pulled the reins of control, and put an end to the relationship.

It had grown dark, and it was time for the meal to conclude. Regina suggested that John show me the sights of Toledo. It was time for her to return to her own family. To my delight, John agreed. We made arrangements for John to come and pick me up at the motel in an hour. I thanked her for arranging our gathering. She indicated she found it very interesting to find out about Don's past, as Don really didn't talk much about it. I was a chapter he hadn't revealed.

My time with John later that night was both insightful as well as emotionally rewarding. John was in his element as we explored the Toledo nightlife. First he probed about what types of places I wanted to see and then put together a plan. Initially, we stopped at a pool bar, which had a wide selection of local microbrews. It was an older establishment, in what I perceived to be in an ethnic neighborhood. We played a game of pool and talked about our lives, our plans, and our childhoods. A deep thinker, John offered many paths to explore our mystical father. John was also interested in what I knew about Don and about my visit with Ina. He had intensions of keeping in contact with her after his initial contact, following the death of his great-aunt Sally. But like many intentions, the letters and calls dissipated as time went on. I had brought what pictures I had gathered, and he seemed to be curious about pictures I had gathered of Don's youth as well as the other Brookshier family members.

We had already drifted off John's plan, as our discussion kept us longer at the first stop. He decided to change the agenda and go to our last planned stop. It was a rehabbed brick building in downtown Toledo. Our dialogue continued, but soon it was time to wrap up the evening. On the way back to my motel, John drove me past Regina's house—the house in which he grew up. It appeared to be a smaller brick ranch, not that much different than the home I grew up in. As we passed it, John commented that he really didn't know much about Don and found as he got older his curiosity about Don grew. He enjoyed getting together since I was as eager to explore who Don was as he was. When he dropped me off at the motel, we agreed to keep in contact, and I agreed to keep him informed on my findings. He was interested to hear what I found out about Ron Bracken and what happened to Don after Regina left.

My trip home was uneventful. I spent much time reflecting on meeting Regina, John, and Guy. Per my overanalytical nature, I neatly sorted out various personality attributes of Don's other sons and classified them into categories of commonalities. I also thought about Regina and what getting to know her told me about Don. He obviously had an appetite for beautiful women. All in all, I decided the trip was worth the time and expense.

It was time for the school year to begin. Despite its slow beginnings, it had been quite a summer. I had found so much, yet I was still yearning for more. I had met half siblings and found my biological mother, but I was still hungry. Teaching high school had become easier, as I started to understand how high school students worked as opposed to middle school students. I was actually anxious to get back to the regular routine of the school year. Just like the students, I needed the structure and sanity of the regular school year. In a way, the thought of structure offered a comfort zone for my loss of identity. I realized my uncertainty had led to internal chaos, and I was not comfortable with chaos.

By this point I had become comfortable with many of the students, and they were no longer my adversaries. I had been open with all my students, and the returning students were familiar with my adventure. Many probed of my progress. The faculty as well, knew of my discovery and most had accepted my lot in life. It felt good to be in a structured place with familiar faces. Sylvia was also grateful to be back in her comfort zone. To her a husband who was lost in a gale storm of emotions and searches had dominated the summer. To get back to her stable, adult comfort zone was a welcomed relief to the turmoil of our household. Our kids certainly didn't understand what was going on. All they believed was Dad found out his mother and father weren't real. Obviously, it wasn't that simple, but in the minds of young children the simplistic is all that really matters.

Their biggest concern at the time was how it would affect their birthday and Christmas present volume.

CHAPTER 4

MILE MARKERS

A DREADFUL TANGENT
(September 2001)

The new school year was dominated by another event: September 11, 2001. I was at school at the time. It was early in the morning when the newsreels started coming through. Everyone became aware of the situation as soon as it started to unfold. Like many, I had become aware of the event by midmorning. Myself as well as most teachers in my school shifted our lesson plans to that of what was being covered by the news and the startling shock of the reality slowly settled in. Soon we all realized it was more than an accidental plane crash into a building. Our world was changing. To everyone, the relevant was no longer relevant. To me, it was the first time since my awakening that my birth status was not the most important part of my life. On Maslow's hierarchy, I fell down a notch. Personal and family safety became the most important focus of my life. Like many others, I ran to the local food store to prepare a box of canned goods in case of a similar attack to my own community. I was scared. It was the start of the war of terror.

Not only did it affect me but it also affected Sylvia. But the impact on her was very different. While I was a hardcore moderate, Sylvia was a staunch liberal Democrat. It became another wedge in our already fragile relationship. My perspective was that of a grave fracture in the political climate of the world. Her perspective was one of an outrageous result of the Bush regime's poor policies. To Sylvia, the anger of a stolen election was escalating into a world catastrophe. Her rage was building, and my lack of judgment was a display of my lack of awareness to what was really going on. To me, the Republicans now had their turn, and while I didn't agree with their policy, our system of balance between political parties was being played. My recent experience with the fallacy of government truth about my own birth record further entrenched my lack of belief in the credibility of either party. Even before this, I had helped vote Ventura into office in the 1996 Minnesota governor's election. I had long been an independent. My discovery seemed to further entrench my independent beliefs.

In the days following 9/11, I retreated to the basement to organize our belongings. Whenever I was in crisis, I sought order. Our basement had been a mess since the day we moved into the house; 9/11 sent me into an organizing frenzy. As I watched the endless news stories about the travesty, I brought new order to our basement as well as my life.

I decided to join the local volunteer fire department. I made my declaration to Sylvia, who distantly agreed that if I wanted to I was more than welcome to. I should have recognized that her expressionless affect during the agreement had nothing to do with her personal feeling. It was only an agreement to get beyond another irrelevant action to contribute to a futile effort against another misdirected cause. At this point neither of us realized the time commitment and its impact on our already fragile marriage. Neither of us realized this decision might be one of the last apples thrown into the apple cart.

Once the initial shock of the falling Twin Towers passed, my mind drifted back to my search. I realized my search had become my routine, and it was no longer something special. It was simply part of my life. It never left my mind and was back to front and center. Sometimes I would get caught in the moment, but for the most part my search and curiosity was foremost on my mind. I was obsessed with finding out everything I could about Don. What happened to him after Regina left him? I needed to know. Yes, the country had entered a new era, but my mind was stuck in my old reality. I wished I could break from it, but I couldn't. I decided I needed to find new routines.

The fire department offered a new routine. Meetings were the second Tuesday of every month, followed by practices on the fourth Thursday. I needed to take firefighting classes, which were offered at the local technical college. The classes were on Wednesdays. Suddenly my evening life became full of a welcomed structured schedule. Diversion was a welcomed relief. It forced me from focusing on what my mind wanted to obsess about. Unfortunately, it was one more thing that took me away from home.

MY FIRST ANNIVERSARY—ALONE
(OCTOBER 2001)

My discovery anniversary came and went. I knew I had covered miles of ground and made much more progress than so many other adoptees. After all, I found my birth mother, identified who my birth father was, and had even met my birth mother and several half siblings. But I was still hungry. Perhaps the late-discovery aspect to my situation fueled my appetite, or maybe it was just part of my nature. I didn't know. All I did know was I had to keep searching. I needed a more substantial foundation to replace the one I lost. I had more clues. I had more leads to follow.

As long as there was a trail, I had to investigate. Many told me to give it up. It was too time consuming, and I was spending too much on phone bills and trips. To me, they might have just as well told me to quit breathing. I couldn't. But life had to go on. I had three younger children and a wife to take care of. I couldn't maintain my life of inward isolation. I had to start living again.

In the early winter of 2001, we trailered our snowmobiles to northern Wisconsin to Matt's and Suzzie's cabin, where we enjoyed cruising the endless web of trails. It was a pivotal point. I loved the isolation and solitude. Sylvia seemed to love the beauty. We decided we would spend the last money from my inheritance to buy a parcel of land in northern Wisconsin. It seemed like a good investment. Land prices seemed to be endlessly heading higher. It would be a good college fund investment for the kids. In the meantime, we could enjoy the solitude and beauty of northern Wisconsin. For me, it also meant a buffer against the war of terror. If we had a cabin up north, we could escape and live off the land. I realized it would be a far-fetched fantasy, but at least it was an option. It would give me a peace of mind. Not only had my own foundation eroded but also the foundation I believed was my safety net—my government. It seemed ironic in the same year I discovered the depth of fallacy of my own personal belief in the safety and credibility of my state, so, too, did my wider safety net of my national government. Suddenly there was no safe haven. It wasn't at a family level, it wasn't at a community level, it wasn't at a state level, and it was no longer in the big picture—a national level. I was alone. The idea of a cabin in the woods, far away from everything, seemed to represent everything my life had become. We started looking for land and a cabin. The apartment building we owned was up for sale; I was making a shift from a public life to a very private, isolated life.

After a prolonged search, we found a place that seemed perfect. It was halfway between Pembine and Niagara, Wisconsin, just south of the Michigan border. Glacial and logging scars dominated the landscape. It was a forty-acre parcel with prominent rock ridges. The valleys had been logged about five years ago. Whereas the tops of the ridges were left unscathed, the valleys were in an earlier regrowth phase due to clear cutting. We purchased it in December 2001. During one of our early visits, we got lost between the rocky ridges. At first it seemed like only a minor amusement, but as darkness began to fall it felt too close to a news headline for comfort. I became scared for my family; I became scared for myself. We were in danger. As we plowed through the entangled thickets of the recently logged valleys from one rocky ridge to the next, it seemed to parallel my own journey. I was not only physically lost but also psychologically lost. I, too, was lost in my own thicket of trying to find a new foundation. I needed to find a new foundation. We needed to find our way back. Finally, we reached a ridge that had the cabin in sight.

It was a thirteen-foot-by-thirteen-foot log cabin with a loft for a sleeping area. An electric well pump called for a generator, which we purchased soon after we acquired the land. There was no electricity, no phone, and no gas. It was the perfect plot of isolation and beauty. One of our original improvements was to add a wood-burning stove. It had a small propane-fired heater, but Sylvia and I both loved the concept of generating our own heat from the land. It also contained a small kitchen area, complete with a nonplumbed sink and a propane-fired oven and stove. We replaced the built-in bunks with a larger loft and futon bed. It would become our sanctuary—our place of escape. Our original intention was to have a place to launch the snowmobiles, but as it grew into its own expression of our life it became something much more significant. It became us.

During the early spring of 2002, Sylvia and I decided to tackle another project together. Our home was without a garage. Its postmodern theme cried for something to complement its contradiction of the past and present. We decided a rehabbed log garage built out of an old log barn would solve many problems. Not only would it give our newer home grounding in history, especially since it was located on Homestead Drive, but it would also give us additional logs to expand our dream in our retreat up north. I was already nervous, as our marriage seemed shaky, especially since my discovery. We committed to see the project through. It was another commitment that wouldn't be fulfilled.

Isolation and beauty also became a theme for the rest of the spring. As beautiful as Sylvia was, she became more isolated as she became more depressed. As for me, I became more isolated. The cabin became my focal point. Summer was approaching, and my search had come to a full-blown standstill. I continued periodic contacts with Maureen, and even Katie, but I couldn't make any headway with my search for Don. Periodically, I would try to find Ron Bracken, or even search for a clue about Edna Owens and her family, but nothing ever surfaced. Edna's family seemed to be very elusive. Similar to Ron, they seemed like people who didn't want to be found. Soon I would be away from access to my T1 line at school and rely upon my antiquated phone line at home.

IN SEARCH OF RON AND EDNA—THE LONG HAUL

My daughters were involved in the 2002 play at the middle school. It was *The Wizard of Oz*. That was another irony. Suddenly Dorothy was thrust into the land of Oz. It was a land unfamiliar to Dorothy, and I felt just like Dorothy. A sudden whirlwind took her away from the comfort of home and dropped her into a new world. It was a complete cast of characters she had never seen before. Such was the fate of my life. I didn't know the new cast, and I certainly didn't know any of the characters. How could I find my way back home? Maybe Professor Marvel could show me the way? I hadn't a clue. All I knew was there was no place like home. I wanted to find home. While I waited for the kids to practice their roles during rehearsals, I used an available computer to conduct family searches.

I decided the only way to find out what happened to Don was to find Ron Bracken. I tried countless internet searches, each time coming up with dozens of Ron Brackens, Ronald Brackens, or R. Brackens. Methodically, relentlessly, I called them. Maybe I would have the same luck as I did in tracking down the Brookshier family. Just maybe the adoption gods would be on my side, and I'd strike it rich. Even if it was a distant cousin, they could send me on a new fresh trail. But I found nothing. No one knew of the Ron Bracken who was born to Edna, with a maiden name of Owens. Every now and then, I would make a potential hit. Some thought they might know who I was talking about but would have to look into it. Eventually, I would call back, and the trail would be cold again. I thought it was possible Edna's death certificate could shed some light. When I received and examined it, there were more potential clues. Lee Hyatt, in Shasta County, California, signed it. It also listed the long-term care facility where Edna died. First I tried the care facility, but due to confidentiality issues they couldn't provide any additional information. Ina told me that Edna had two other children from a man with the last name Hyatt. I decided Lee must be one of Edna's other children. I started searching for Lee in Shasta County. Once again the trail grew cold. I had found a Lee Hyatt, but she had moved, with no forwarding information.

One evening I decided to try a new combination in a search for Tex Owens, Don's uncle. After combing through the first page of references to the Grand Ole Opry and music stores that offered his CD, I happened upon a reference to a website titled "Descendants of Joseph Owens." The reference suggested that some of the postings were from his family members. I decided to investigate. When I tried to access the website, I found I couldn't get in, because I wasn't an established member. The denial message contained the name and email address of the website manager, Vernon Hord. I contacted Vernon and explained my situation. Vernon responded immediately. He was more than willing to accommodate my curiosity. He seemed to be the portal I was looking for.

Along with a membership to the Owens family site, he also provided a password for the Sunday family site. The Sundays were an old Pensacola, Florida, family, from which some of the Owens were descended. Once again I found a gold mine. The Descendants of Joseph Owens website was a genealogical dream come true. It contained pictures and family trees that extended back to the 1600s. The Owens had been in the United States as long as the Brookshiers. Don was from a very old southern family. It was another identity to try on.

I spent the next several weeks combing through the site and exploring the various branches of the Owens's and Sunday's family trees. The vast majority of the branches led to the British Isles, with a periodic northern European stray. It also contained pictures of Edna and her family. Edna was from a family of twelve brothers and sisters. Someone had posted a picture of Edna's entire immediate family standing on the front porch of their Oklahoma home. In addition to Tex Owens, the site contained information about Edna's sister, Texas Ruby. Texas Ruby had married a fiddle player, Curley Fox, who made radio stardom during the 1940s and 1950s. It appeared Edna had followed a career path familiar to her family. Additionally, the site contained many pictures and postings documenting the family's rich tapestry within American history. The Civil War, the War of 1812, the Mexican-American War, and more blood tracing back to the American Revolution were now part of my history. It was another irony. Sylvia was from a family that dated back to the Revolutionary War. Now I, too, had a rich American historical root. I was amazed and humbled by my discovery. I even found a noble Scottish root. I had missed the Scots since I fell from the Lennox family tree. I was in awe.

It turned out Edna's mother, Susan Francis Owens, was the ancestor who tied the Owens and Sundays together. Her mother was Charlotte Sunday. It was on the Sunday site that I was able to trace the roots back to the Dunham Castle, in Scotland. To save the life of the Dunham family line during an upheaval in seventeenth-century Scotland, Joseph Single-ton was smuggled on to a freight ship sailing to America with a servant. Joseph was never again to see his family or homeland. I felt a kindred spirit to Joseph Singleton, as we had both been sent away to save our lives. Had I known in high school what I knew now, I am certain I would have found American history much more interesting.

While the website contained a treasure's worth of information about the Owens family and its history, it only contained one line item referencing Ron and Don. It merely acknowledged they were the issue of Edna. My search for Ron, and ultimately Don, had once again come to a dead end. I resorted again to periodically trying random calls to the hundreds of R., Ron, and Ronald Brackens. Verizon loved me.

During the summer of 2002, Sam, Ellen's husband, and I made frequent trips up to the cabin to make improvements. We added an outhouse as well as a proposed sauna. I added trails through the land. I realized it was like my path through the chaos of my heritage. As I spent time cutting new trails, I paralleled them to the trails I had cut though my biological past. Each branch and trunk I cut was like another family member I found. Endlessly I forged my way through an undiscovered land. Yet my thirst remained unquenched. I needed to forge further. I needed to cut more trails.

As the weather grew hotter during the summer, my search trails grew colder. I was getting nowhere, another school year had started, and the second anniversary of my discovery came and went. Periodically, I thought about hiring a private investigator to find out more about Don's life, but I was afraid I would just fall prey to a money-hungry vulture waiting to clean out the monetary carcass of another victim. My level of mistrust in humanity was escalating. So was my consumption of alcohol as I visited abandon land, my newfound metaphorical place, where I would dwell on the potential effects of feeling like a discarded being. I couldn't face my reality.

Another fall had settled in, and I decided to make a desperate attempt to find anyone who could actually connect me with Ron. I knew the Descendants of Joseph Owens website had some subscribers who came out of the same branch of the family tree as Edna, since there was the picture posted of Edna and her family. I must be at least distantly related to someone who posted on the site; however, I didn't recognize any of the names. I thought if I just posted a note indicating I was looking for offspring of Edna, the elusive Owens I was looking for wouldn't surface. So I decided to post one of the pictures I had gotten from Ina. It was a picture of Edna, with Don sitting on her lap. Don couldn't have been older than six in the picture. The caption posted with the picture read: "Edna Owens with Don Brookshier, my grandmother and father." It worked. Two days later I received an email: "My name is Pat Allen, and I'm confused. Edna was my mother, and Don was my brother. Who are you?" I quickly emailed her back, indicating who I was, and I described my situation. The next day she responded, saying I should call her. She wanted to talk to me.

I called her as soon as the school day was over. Pat was unaware of my existence, but she did know of Don's two other sons. She was very interested in my plight and eager to help me. Pat Allen was Don's oldest sister, from Edna's second marriage to Cecil Hyatt. She said she had one sister, Lee, who was about two years younger than her, which aligned with Regina's description of Don's family. She further added that Edna divorced Cecil and subsequently married a man named Boyd Bracken, to whom she bore a son, Ron. Edna actually divorced Boyd, but she later remarried him before he died, and she became a widow, perhaps for the second time in her life. Apparently, multiple marriages were common in the Owens clan. Pat believed one of Edna's sisters, Milly, had divorced as many as fifteen times. This was turning out to be a very interesting family. Pat and I talked for about an hour, and she was able to fill in many of the missing pieces concerning Edna and her family. She also told me about her children. She had been married twice and was now divorced from her most recent husband. Through the unions, she had three children. Her children included an older boy and two younger girls.

Unfortunately, Pat hadn't seen or heard from Don since the early 1980s. She indicated that he basically disappeared—she believed it was around the time Regina left him. Pat also indicated that Edna had wondered about him for quite some time. She was aware of his death. Ron had told her. That led to the question of how I could get in contact with Ron. After all, since he had signed Don's death certificate, he might have a clue about what happened to Don between the time Regina left and his death in 1993. As we were talking, I felt my adrenaline rushing. I was finally getting close to finding out about Don's missing years. After two years of searching, I would finally have a resolution.

But I hit a brick wall. Following Edna's death, Pat and her siblings parted ways. As far as she was concerned, they were no longer family. She didn't know what happened to Ron or Lee, and she wasn't interested in finding out. I could tell by her tone this was a raw nerve, and I best not dig too deep, or she might cut my contact with her short. After all, she seemed to be very nice, and she had already provided so many answers. Maybe with time she would soften and help me find Ron. She agreed to send me copies of whatever photos she had of Edna, Lee, Ron, and herself. I told her I would send photos of myself as well as my family. She didn't have many; it turned out Lee got most of what Edna had when she died. We agreed to keep in contact.

Christmas was around the corner. Once again I had another Christmas to be thankful for. After all, I was finally living my life. I now knew I was adopted and had found so much about my biological family. I had my own wonderful family. I had a job I enjoyed and friends who would listen to me. Based on my belief structure, I had everything I could be thankful for. I even sent a poinsettia to my biological mother, and my kids received cards and a popcorn tin from Maureen. Yet I thought of the Christmas I buried Nic. I didn't blame him, but I missed him. He had been a great father. It was the time of year when I remembered him. I always thought it's unfortunate that people seemed to remember the dead by how they were when they died, not how they lived. I constantly tried to remember his life, but it was his death that naturally came to mind.

We decided to spend our first New Year's in the cabin. It would be a great opportunity to get the kids away from the commercialism of New Year's and have some quality family time together. Even though there was little snow in southern Wisconsin that New Year's, there was plenty up at the cabin. We brought snow toys. The snowmobiles were a necessity, since the last couple of miles into the cabin weren't plowed. There was a smaller hill on our land upon which the kids could ride snow tubes. I spent endless hours helping the kids getting their tubes and saucers up and down the hill. I was also able to take the kids on rides around the old logging trails. It was a beautiful winter wonderland. On New Year's Eve, we found a restaurant just south of the Michigan border that offered a New Year's lobster buffet. While Sylvia and I feasted on the lobster delicacy, the kids found happiness in a multitude of action video games. I felt distance from my adoption issues. Sylvia also seemed to find comfort in a break from the daily labor of our home.

PART II

NEW CRISES, NEW LIVES,
NEW ROUTINES

CHAPTER 5

GRACE'S CRISIS

MARCH 2003

My search had become stale and boring. Even though Pat had become a dead end, she managed to surprise me by sending me a crocheted blanket Edna had made for Don. It was one of the few possessions she had from Edna's estate. To me, it was an incredible emotional tie to my biological past, and I was extremely grateful. Beyond that, I really didn't advance much. I continued to have periodic communications with Maureen, Katie, and my half brother John. As time went on, my contacts with both John and Guy seemed to fall by the wayside. In the meantime, my ties with my adoptive family seemed to normalize. We had reached a détente. If I didn't bring up the adoption issue, they would interact with me. It's not that I really minded the diminishing intensity; it seemed to be something that was needed, especially for my relationship with Sylvia.

As for Sylvia and me, we seemed to be drifting further and further apart. I had been taking my firefighting classes, but they, too, seemed to be endless. Sylvia had grown tired of the relentless routine of school each day, followed by a night of carting kids around, and the intensity of kids trying to settle into their nighttime winding-down period. My preoccupation and anger exacerbated her uneasiness with our relationship. We had moved from a union of marriage to two individual paths, neither of which seemed to have much in common. I hated her indifference; she hated my solitude. The kids seemed oblivious to our struggles.

During mid-February 2003, we were all starting to feel the cooped-up cabin fever feeling common to the final stretches of a long Wisconsin winter. All we needed was a break—something to relieve the doldrums of what had become an eternal winter of stress. Sylvia and I decided it would be good to make another trip up north in late winter with some friends of ours. We planned a snowmobile weekend with Jim, Lisa, and their kids. Lisa booked the rooms at a place with a pool, just outside Crivitz, Wisconsin. Jim and Lisa had two boys. The oldest was the same age as my oldest, Grace, and the youngest was the same age as my youngest, Tony. We had previously enjoyed many camping trips and weekend campfires together, which seemed to indicate the kids would get along fine. Jim owned a local auto service center, which I used, and was a strong advocate of a better technical education program in the school. Jim and I enjoyed many conversations that emphasized the need for practical skills within the schools. Sylvia also enjoyed Lisa's company. It sounded like the perfect winter getaway. We planned it for late February, when the snow was deep, and the weather was just starting to warm up.

On Friday night, we met Jim, Lisa, and the kids at the motel. The Crivitz Inn was donut shaped, with a pool enclosed in the center. Our rooms were adjoining, and soon the kids were in their own world of running between the rooms while we enjoyed poolside cocktails. It seemed like the perfect respite. Eventually, it was time to quit the constant feed of quarters to the arcade next to the pool and rest for the upcoming day of snowmobiling. We had a trailer for Tony, which he could share with

Remington, the youngest of Jim and Lisa. Anticipation filled the air. The following day was supposed to be a perfect snowmobiling day, as the forecast indicated it would make it into the midforties by the end of the day. We determined if we started early we could have hours of snowmobile heaven before the trails softened. We enjoyed a restful night's sleep. It would be our last for some time.

The sleds were unloaded and ready to go by eight, after a good old-fashioned country breakfast at a nearby cafe. There was a slight mist in the air as the temperature started to climb. Northern Wisconsin had wonderful trails. Nestled among the pine, spruce, and hardwood forests, the trails wound endlessly through hills and ravines, over creeks, and across barren lakes. Eagles soared as the whine of two-cycle engines ripped around curves that revealed breathtaking panoramas. We truly were in snowmobile heaven.

After a couple of hours, we took a break and ate the lunch we had packed. The kids romped in the snow as Sylvia, Jim, Lisa, and I basked in the glory of a successful family outing. Unfortunately, the way home didn't follow the anticipated ending. The sunbaked trails had turned to glaze in the shadows of the woodlands, and one missed turn changed our lives. Grace, my oldest, met her fate with a tree. A snowmobile accident would take our lives into uncharted territory. Her stomach hurt, and she grew weak. We decided I would take her back as the others tended to the wrecked snowmobile. As I raced back to our vehicles with her on my snowmobile, I prayed for her survival. I could tell it was more than a simple stomachache.

By the time we arrived back to our truck, Grace seemed to be coming around. She just wanted to rest in the back seat for a while. I wasn't sure what to think, but I could hear the snowmobiles with the others not far behind. When they arrived, Grace was sleeping but could awake easily when prompted. The snowmobile needed work, but it wasn't anything that couldn't be fixed. We loaded up and decided to get a bite to eat on the way back to the motel. Jim and Lisa knew of a place close by they had frequented. Grace seemed to be perking up. She was hungry and wanted a kiddy cocktail. It seemed like a good sign. We all thought the crisis had passed.

Jim and Lisa were right. The place idealized the perfect northern Wisconsin supper club. Located on a lake, it offered beautiful vistas with a full range of video games inside. It would be the perfect place to reminisce and reflect on the day's events. At first Grace seemed to be getting livelier by the minute. Quarters and kiddy cocktails were her only concern. But soon events took a dark turn. Her stomach was hurting again. She wanted to sit at the table. Her head went down on the table. She threw up. Sylvia grew deeply concerned. Everyone understood this was something that needed immediate attention. Grace was going downhill fast. The closest emergency room was in Marinette, Wisconsin, about an hour away. Jim and Lisa would take Madeline and Tony back to the motel with their kids, and Sylvia and I would run Grace over to Marinette to have her checked out.

The drive was agonizing. Minutes seemed like hours. Grace wanted to sleep, but we were afraid to let her lose consciousness. An endless web of backcountry roads eventually led us to the county highway system. Grace was getting worse by the second, and every new stretch of highway seemed to take hours to complete. The triage nurse at the emergency room seemed to understand the gravity of the situation and quickly escorted us into an exam room, where the attending physician was waiting. He was concerned. When asked family history questions, a new complication arose. We were in the dark. Aside from Maureen's genetic disease, my entire medical history was not mine. It was fabricated. The doctor determined she needed additional testing. She needed an MRI. Sylvia and I waited.

It was as he feared. She had a fractured spleen. It was a level four, with level five being the worst. She needed immediate surgery to remove her spleen, or her internal bleeding would kill her. He told us had we not brought her in that night she most likely would have died by morning. I was scared. He called the surgeon. We waited.

When the surgeon arrived, he concurred. She was in grave danger. Unfortunately, at her young age, there were significant consequences to having her spleen removed. The spleen was an adjacent organ to the liver and functioned to regenerate blood cells. As an adult, one could live without it fairly comfortably, but as an adolescent it would mean a regimen of drugs, with side effects, until she was about twenty. What did we want to do? Sylvia and I had both worked in health care prior to teaching, so we knew there were always options. When asked about other options, the surgeon balked. If it were his child, he would put her on a wait-and-see scenario. Like livers, spleens are remarkable organs, often capable of healing themselves. In the right setting, we could have her monitored over the next several weeks in intensive care to see if the spleen would repair itself. If it took a turn for the worse, it could be removed. Unfortunately, the hospital in Marinette wasn't the right place to do that. Green Bay, Wisconsin, would be the closest. She would have to use the flight for life helicopter to transport her to Saint Vincent Hospital, where they had the necessary facilities and equipment. Even with that option, there was a risk we could lose her during the flight. I further probed if one of us could go with her on the helicopter ride down to Green Bay. That wasn't an option. There just wasn't enough room. She could die, and neither of us would be there with her. That was our only option. Sylvia and I talked and decided it was worth the try.

We watched the helicopter take off from the pad after Grace was loaded. The drive to Green Bay was agonizing. On the way Sylvia and I tried to keep a positive attitude as we battled between blame and optimism. I was the one who brought snowmobiling into our lives. If I hadn't done that, Grace wouldn't be in this situation. Was it my fault? Isn't that what every parent asks when they see their child in peril? What did I do wrong? I prayed to whatever God was listening, "Please help this child." She didn't need to die as a result of my selfishness. Was she dying because I had been too selfish by trying to find my roots? Everything was on the table. I was willing to give up everything just to save her life. I didn't really need to know who I was; I just needed her to live. I didn't care. I would make my deal with God; I would make my deal with the devil. I just wanted her to have a chance to live her life.

As Sylvia and I passed the ninety-minute drive to Saint Vincent's Hospital, we moved passed blame and into gratefulness. At that point, despite our marital differences, we found common ground. We wanted Grace to live. We wanted her to have a chance for her own life, despite our issues. We talked intimately, perhaps for the first and last time in a long while. We fought, we cried, we even laughed. Grace was the only thing on our minds. The road was dark and vacant. Nobody else seemed to be on the endless stretch of highway on which we were trapped. In retrospect, it was one of the few times in over two years it didn't feel like I was adopted. It didn't matter.

The directions the hospital in Marinette gave us were good. They brought us directly to the emergency room of Saint Vincent's Hospital in Green Bay. I dropped Sylvia off and found the first parking spot. Was she still alive? I didn't know. I ran into the emergency room and asked the triage nurse where to find my family. She seemed calm and gave me directions, so I assumed Grace was still alive. When I arrived in the room, Grace was awake and chatty. She was nervous about getting yet another IV line. I was relieved. God had answered my prayers. My precious daughter's life had been spared. There was hope. Little did I know, it was only another beginning.

Time in the ER was short. She was quickly taken up to the pediatric intensive care unit, where her vital signs would be monitored. The plan was to wait and watch her for the next six weeks. If her vital signs took a dip, she would have another MRI to determine if her spleen was failing. If so, it would be removed. If she made it through the six weeks without a crisis, it meant her spleen was healing. Her hospital stay would be followed by another six months of bed rest to light activity at home. We understood the plan but didn't understand the hardship it would bring. Sylvia and I agreed to a split schedule. Green Bay was an hour from our home. We each would make a trade-off between two and three days in Green Bay on weekdays and split the weekends. Grace was our number-one priority at this point.

I ran back to Crivitz to pick up our belongings as well as Madeline and

Tony. Sylvia would take the first watch, and I would come back Monday morning so she could return to get her classes in order, and make substitute plans for the early part of the week. It wasn't an ideal plan, but it had to work. Over the next several weeks, some of Grace's friends came to visit. Madeline and Tony found comfort in seeing Grace during our trade-offs of responsibility. Grace's classmates sent a package of get well cards. The abnormal once again became our routine.

After four weeks Grace's MRI revealed her spleen was healing remarkably well, and the doctor indicated it would be safe for her to return to home for a week or two of bed rest. Once she returned to school, she would need to be on a modified bed rest schedule. Gym, recess, or any other physical activity would not be allowed. We were just glad to get her home, and end our weekly ritual of traveling back and forth to Green Bay. Both Sylvia and I had burned up most of our allotted sick days. But that didn't seem to matter; Grace was healing. Eventually, it was time for Grace to return to home. Even though her routine hadn't drastically changed, she was at least in the comfort of her home. Sylvia and I had brought her books and games to play, but she soon became sick of living a solitary lifestyle.

CHAPTER 6

A LITTLE TOO LITTLE, A LITTLE TOO LATE

APRIL 2003

The newest crisis in my life was coming to an end. It had an effect to what I imagined electroshock therapy created, and my inward spiral had been abruptly thwarted. While my conscious thoughts would periodically drift back to my adoption search and grappling with a new identity as an adoptee, it was no longer a consuming obsession. It was time to focus on pulling my life with my family back together. Grace's accident had taken all of us on an emotional roller-coaster ride, and we all seemed a little lost. The school year was dragging through the long winter stretch as we all longed for a relaxing spring break. Although Sylvia and I had actually been away from school quite a bit during the last month, the ordeal was exhausting, and we were both burnt out. Both Madeline and Tony also felt the stress of living in a single-parent family, as either Sylvia or I were always gone during the previous month. While it seemed we all pulled together, it soon became apparent Grace's spleen wasn't the only fracture in our family. Our family structure had also fractured.

I made a commitment to myself that I would do the best I could to ease the building tension in my marriage and back down whenever things started to heat up between Sylvia and myself. I thought I was doing better, but Sylvia didn't seem to notice, as she continued to retreat. The time I spent volunteering for the fire department in training and monthly meetings, along with the required class work at the local community college, took me away from home more than she could tolerate. To her, I was never around. To me, whenever I left, the house fell apart, and I returned only to clean up another mess. Despite my effort to try to bring down the stress level, the tension seemed to be rising by the minute.

April 1, 2003, brought my forty-fourth birthday. I had developed a taste for contemporary country western music. This had been a drastic change from the "angry man" metal rock music I turned to following my mother's death. As events unfolded, the anger that seemed to fuel the dark rock music seemed to be a perfect fit to my newly acquired bastard nation split personality. Since Grace's recovery, however, my anger had been tempered by my gratefulness. The peaceful reflective melodies of Tim McGraw that rambled through my head seemed to steer me in a new direction. For my birthday Sylvia gave me a Tim McGraw CD. To me, it was meaningful in that it was full of love songs. To her, it was just something she thought was my newest fad.

Six days later my world turned upside down again. Sylvia told me she was leaving. I didn't understand. Where was she going? Why was she telling me this? I could tell by the somber expression on her face this was something more than a trip to the grocery store. She was moving into an apartment. She was lost and unable to make decisions. She had thought it through and decided she needed to find herself. The only way she could regain herself was through quiet isolation and solitude. She decided she would get an apartment in Cedar Grove, where I taught and the kids attended school, to diminish the impact on the kids. We would split the time with the kids—one week with me, followed by a week with her. Her decision was final.

I was in shock. Initially, I questioned her sanity, as I tried to grapple with the implications. This came out of nowhere. Yes, we were having marital problems, but it seemed to me most people were, at least to some degree. Was it the adoption thing? How could she blame me for that? I had nothing to do with it. What about the kids? How could we do this to them? Not only were there Madeline and Tony, who would experience the trauma of divorce, but also Grace, who had not yet fully recovered from her spleen accident. How could she do this to us? Our house was in the middle of a garage construction project, and in bad need of a paint job. There was no way it was ready for the market. Once again I seemed to be the only one in the dark. But in reality, her world had also turned dark. According to her new views, there was never a good moment in our marriage. She didn't love me now, and in retrospect she never did. I was arrogant. I was self-centered. I had a volatile, unpredictable temper. I was the cause of everything bad in our lives, and she needed to get away. She wanted to be out as soon as possible.

Perhaps from Sylvia's perspective this was a normal part of life. It wasn't a life she chose, but simply a life she had been born into. She had been from a split family; her family did exactly what she was doing. Her mother and father had separated when she was roughly Grace's age. The marriage had been failing, and her mother believed separation needed to happen. But theirs was an unusual separation. Chuck, Sylvia's father, and Sarah, Sylvia's mother, agreed to live independent lives, but there was still an intermingling of their lives as parents. Even though Chuck lived with his new girlfriend, Chuck came home for supper almost every night. It was a time when Sylvia acquired a half sister. It was a weird twist of fate that allowed Sylvia and me to share another commonality. We both had half siblings.

While Sylvia was accustomed to a split family, it was not my norm. I was raised in an intact family. My parents weren't perfect. I eventually suspected there were extramarital affairs, but they stayed together. Whether it was because the loved each other in a way I didn't understand, or they stayed together for the sake of the commitment they made together, adopting me, I'll never know. But I do know they stayed together. Little did they know, the kids always know. I long suspected they were in a dishonest marriage, but I never let my secret known. I found it appalling that Sylvia would want to bring our marital problems public and actually move out. To her, it was the natural thing to do. It was the honest thing to do. Once again our differences became apparent.

As the moment passed, another reality hit. How could she do this to me? We made our vows and promised faithfulness through thick and thin. Maybe it was thin, but didn't the vow count for anything? I had been in peril for the last several years; first with my father's death, followed by my mother's death, and finally the adoption revelation. If nothing else, couldn't she see the last thing I needed was another loss, another rejection at this time in my life? I felt dejected; I felt betrayed.

Did I love her? I just didn't know. I knew the last several years had been hard, and I felt she had been unfair to me. But I didn't think I deserved this. God, I had been through so much. How could she do this to me? Yes, she also suffered as a result of my discovery. After all, she thought she was married and bore children to a Romanian, German, and Polish husband, and suddenly none of that was true. Was that a clause in our marriage vows I missed? Maybe there was an asterisk. Maybe it stated: "As long as all assumptions are true." After all, I apparently wasn't who I was when we married. Even our children weren't who we both thought they were. Suddenly, in an instant, they went from being eastern European to mostly British Islander and Norwegian. To me, none of that mattered in the context of marriage vows. Apparently, it did.

Yet Sylvia persisted. According to her, the adoption had little to do with her decision. It was more who I was. She just wasn't in love with me anymore. The implications of what it could do to our children were irrelevant; she just knew she couldn't live with me anymore. Furthermore, the reasons were also irrelevant; it was more an issue of feeling. She didn't necessarily want a divorce; she just wanted to be separated. She wanted to live in a separate home. It was something she needed. I tried to understand what she needed, but at that time, I just couldn't understand. To me, she was being selfish. She was only thinking about what she needed, beyond the community that was our family. To me, she wanted a divorce. I started to get angry.

Failure of a marriage brings a multitude of feelings. To the spouse out of control, the grieving process is real. The first feeling is denial. Initially, I thought this wasn't happening. It's not that I thought she hadn't said what she said, but it was more that I thought she didn't mean what she said. I didn't think she really meant she wanted to split up; she just needed me to pay more attention to what she thought. I was wrong. She meant what she said. To me, she had to have lost her mind or she wouldn't be doing what she was doing. Didn't she realize, once one of us went down this path, it was fatal. I couldn't imagine, or I should say comprehend, the thought of once one partner went to the extent of moving out and actually saying they didn't love the other; there was any hope for saving the marriage. To me, my parents never pursued that path in their marriage, so I wasn't capable of seeing once the marriage had gotten to that point; there was any other direction beyond a final divorce. I thought Sylvia must really be losing her mind, or she wouldn't be saying such crazy things. She needed to see a counselor, if not for the sake of our marriage, but for the sake of her being able to take care of the children when they would be under her care.

I didn't see the magnitude of the problem. It was still her problem, not mine. On the other hand, from her perspective at the time, the problem was mine. Each of us blaming the other wasn't conducive to solving the problem. All I knew is, this couldn't happen. Not only for the kid's sake but also this couldn't happen for me. I wasn't sure how this would play into my recent experience with destruction of trust. My parents had lied to me. My relatives had lied to me. Even the state, to whom I faithfully paid taxes, lied to me. And now I also was finding out my trust in my spouse held as much credibility as that of my government and my raised family. Promises were meant to be broken. Nobody was to be trusted. I had lost trust in my past. But now Sylvia was shattering my trust in my present and my future. What was my future outside of my children? I had lived the past eleven years as a family man, and now my family was disintegrating. Without a past, a present, or a future, what was left? I wasn't sure anymore.

I reflected during that day and the following day, Sunday. Maybe I should have seen this coming. As we drifted apart, she grew closer to a friend I had introduced her to, Susan Rile. I met Susan during one of Tony's parent lunches I attended. While the kids were playing, following the lunch, I struck up a conversation with Susan, who was watching her daughter, Emma. As we talked, I discovered she was from the East Coast and was Irish. Those were two of Sylvia's strongest prides. Something told me the two of them would hit it off, so I decided they had to meet. Sylvia seemed starved for friendships following our move from Minnesota. As we talked further, I also discovered they lived fairly close to us, so I made arrangements for the two to meet. I was right: they hit it off immediately.

Susan's husband was originally from England, and they had met during mutual employment on a cruise ship. She was a singer, and he played in the band. Susan had a degree in music, and David's was in horticulture. While his degree didn't get him onto the cruise ship, it did eventually land him a job selling bulb plants for a Dutch company in the area. They previously lived in New Hampshire but moved to Wisconsin to be closer to Susan's family. They had four children, who were close in ages to our children. It seemed to be another match that helped our families click. At the time the budding friendship seemed to solve so many problems. It turned out that their friendship had grown far beyond my original intentions. Susan was the friend Sylvia initially went with to look for apartments. I had been clueless.

As I struggled with her decision during that very long day, I tried to come to the realization she had made her mind up, and this was going to happen. Even though reality seemed undeniable, I still clung to my cloak of denial. I was good at denial. The next day I sought the advice of our high school counselor, Sue. Sue had been through a divorce, and she was one of the few people in the area who might be able to offer some solid advice. She recommended Dr. Trott.

Dr. Trott was a marriage counselor she had seen at a recent seminar who was well regarded in the marriage reconciliation circuit. When I called him, he suggested we arrange a meeting based on the assumption of trying to have the best possible split for the kids. He also recommended I suggest to Sylvia that we try to postpone the actual split until the end of the school year, in the best interest of the kids. It would give them the summer break to adjust to the concept of us splitting up. I suggested his plan to Sylvia, and she reluctantly agreed to give it a try.

The remaining days of the school year were spent with endless emails to Sylvia trying to convince her my love was worthy as well as to attend weekly marriage counseling sessions. While it periodically seemed like we were making progress, it also seemed like we had many setbacks. The most notable sign was the on-again, off-again wedding ring. I could always tell exactly how she was really feeling by looking to see if her wedding ring was still on her finger. Sometimes it would be there, but before I knew it, it would disappear. Whenever it was gone, I knew she was focusing on moving out again. I cried. I pleaded. I even tried romancing her by a surprise trip to our honeymoon location for a dinner. We had spent our honeymoon in a quaint resort area located about ninety minutes north of our home. But it was all to no avail. The end of the school year came, and she signed a lease. I had the first week with the kids as she settled in. I was shocked. In our final counseling session before she moved, the counselor suggested not many couples reconcile after one partner has physically moved out. I still was in denial. I was devastated. I was hurt.

LIFE IN THE BALANCE
(MAY 2003)

My reality was crashing in. I knew I needed to balance the bad with something good. Somehow I needed to bring balance into this travesty. I had already started to accept the identity of a rejected soul as I internalized my birth status, but this seemed to seal my fate. Was I trash, something to be thrown away? How could I balance this with something good enough to keep me in check? We had recently started snowmobiling, which I really enjoyed. It brought me great sorrow when Grace had her accident, but I really liked the feeling of getting out, winding up the engine, and exploring uncharted territory. I decided I would try the summertime equivalent; I would learn to ride a motorcycle. I would buy a Harley.

I had never ridden before, so for me this was a new idea. I told Sylvia of my intention, and as predicted she didn't seem to care. I wasn't looking for a reaction, but given our upcoming divorce I wanted to make sure she was aware of how I was spending our money. The odd thing was that Sylvia didn't really seem interested in the monetary aspects of our separation. I had inherited a sizable sum of money upon my mother's death. It's not that it was enough for us to retire on, but it was enough to matter in the case of divorce. It was enough to fight over. But she wasn't fighting.

Given my reality, I didn't want her to have my parents' money. My father had earned it, and my mother, based on their decision, left it to me. As Sylvia was the one who was pushing for our impending divorce, I didn't think my parents would have wanted her to have it. At the time Chic died, our marriage was already somewhat shaky. My mother had designated me as executor of her will, but since we lived in Minnesota, and she died in Wisconsin, the state decided I couldn't be executor. The state indicated they were too afraid I would take the money, leave town, and skip any unclaimed expenses. As a lawyer, my uncle Bob agreed to be the executor pro bono. He was Chic's brother. I was miffed, but I agreed. Despite his culpability in the family lie of my birth status, Bob seemed trustworthy. I thought I could trust him with this, so I thought it was a good option.

Bob had always been an important part of my life. His views helped shape many of my political beliefs. My mother's family was split. Many rumors circulated among family members as to why and how Chic's mother, Marie, actually died. The given cause on the death certificate was complications from surgery. Chic was the younger of the two sisters; Irene was her older sister. Joseph, Chic's father, was a union breaker during the Depression. Maybe it wasn't honorable, but it gave his family a living during tough times. When Marie died, Joseph married Ann, who had four boys. Chic's family seemed to split right between the twins, who were in the middle of the four boys. During most of the time I was growing up, there seemed to be strife in her family. They were a loud, gregarious people. Holidays were heartfelt, with many discussions ending in, "You son of a bitch." Bob was the younger of the twins, and Rich was the eldest. Both Bob and Rich were the only two in the family to earn bachelor degrees. Bob still needed more, and eventually earned both a master's and a Juris Doctor.

Both Bob and Rich were in the army, and many stories circulated about who screwed up more. Eventually, when they were discharged, Rich took center spotlight in the family when he brought back from Holland the woman of his dreams, Betty, and started a family in Milwaukee. It even made the *Milwaukee Journal Sentinel*. Bob eventually married a woman named Dorothy. While she was intelligent and interesting, she always seemed to struggle to fit into the family. Lester was the eldest son and became an electrician. Les, in many ways was definitely the most laid back in the crowd. It wasn't that he didn't hold his own in the family's holiday shouting matches but Les never seemed to take it to heart. He never carried a chip and didn't seem to get wrapped up in the political struggles of the family. Les worked at Miller Brewery and always seemed to have a spare case of beer for me when I returned from college. The youngest brother was Joe. Joe was by far the youngest and only six years older than I was. Growing up with an uncle six years older than oneself leads to more confrontations than moments of endearment. While I was the eldest of the cousins on my mother's side, Joe always kept me in check.

As Bob and I went through the iterations of resolving the estate, I talked to him about the uncertainty of our marriage, and he suggested on a personal side that he understood, as he faced similar circumstances with his second wife. Going into the marriage, he brought a fair amount of money into their relationship. But he suggested if I loved Sylvia maybe it was worth an investment in trust to place the monies I had gotten from the estate as I wanted, as opposed to strategically placing it based on legal ramifications. I followed his advice. Not so much from a legal perspective, but more from the views of a trusted uncle and a friend.

We were living in Minnesota at the time, and I desperately wanted to move back to southeastern Wisconsin. I had done well in the Twin Cities, but I missed my family and old friends. Sylvia, on the other hand, loved her job, and given the uncertainty of our marriage she didn't want to move. I decided a compromise would be to buy a summer home with the inheritance from my parents in southeastern Wisconsin. She could hold on to her job, and we could spend much time during holidays and in the summer visiting family and friends. When I proposed my idea to Sylvia, she seemed to think it was a good idea. After all, it was a way to get around the stalemate in our marriage.

Originally, we spent a lot of the time that summer looking for a property on the western side of the Milwaukee metro, where there were many inland lakes. I also had some friends who lived in that area. As we toured the dilapidated shacks on channels within our price range and observed the overcrowded conditions of the Milwaukee metro western lakes, we eventually came to the conclusion we should try looking elsewhere. I suggested we look on the north shore of Lake Michigan. Prices seemed to be lower, and both Bob and Joe, along with some friends, lived in the area. Eventually, we found a place in our price range we liked and bought it. It wasn't what we had in mind, but it seemed to be a good place for the price. It was the home that eventually helped drive us apart.

In the back of my mind, I always held on to the possibility that once Sylvia spent some time there she might feel more comfortable with a permanent move. Halfway through the first year, Sylvia suggested she could permanently move to the Lake House. The shores of Lake Michigan reminded her of our honeymoon, and she loved the beauty of the lake property. Even though our lot was fairly narrow, we had vacant land to the south, and the neighbor's house to the north was located very close to the lake. We were set back from the lake and close to the road. The effect was an isolated paradise.

My fantasy dream had worked. Within the first year, Sylvia decided she could make the move. I didn't have to lose my family to live where I wanted. But now it looked like I would lose them anyway. Nearly four years had passed since I thought I had found a path to save our marriage, and now, I was further in the hole. This time, she actually was leaving.

Was I trying to lick my wounds with a Harley? I was from Milwaukee and grew up in the shadow of a Harley Davidson plant. For quite some time I envied the mysterious black-clothed bikers who rumbled past me as I drove my minivan. Every time they passed I couldn't help but noticing myself turning my head in their direction, wondering, *Who were they?* I now knew I wasn't who I thought I was. Maybe I was one of them. I didn't know it, but at this point I knew it was something I had to explore. In addition, my last four years of teaching small engine repair began to infuse my veins with gasoline. I was becoming a junky. Two- and four-cycle engines seemed to match the rhythm of my heartbeat. I loved the smell of two-cycle engine exhaust and appreciated the beauty of a four stroke. I looked like a biker, with my larger, muscular stature, tattoos, and bald head. Why wasn't I a biker? I wasn't sure. I scoured the paper and eventually found a Dyna Glide that sounded perfect. Dyna Glides fell somewhere between the agility of the racing-inspired Sportster line and the comfort of the touring models. After many discussions with friends who had owned bikes, I decided on a Dyna. It would be the perfect starter bike for me. Given my wife's anticipated departure, my fate was sealed. I had turned a corner.

Given my inability to ride the bike I just purchased, I arranged to have it delivered to my home. It arrived the first weekend after Sylvia had left— the end of the last week I was living full time with my kids. The timing couldn't have been better. A friend of mine in the community had recently gone through a split and had previously ridden a Harley. His was a Soft Tail, but the basic operation of the two were the same, so I asked him to come over and give me a lesson on its basic operations. I had already passed my test for a temporary license, so I was street legal. I just didn't know what to do. He agreed to arrive shortly after Sylvia departed for her first night away with the kids. It seemed like the perfect distraction to the horror my life was about to become. I didn't want her to leave. I didn't want my kids to experience the slice of life they were about to. But I had no control over the situation.

Getting my first lesson on my new Harley seemed to be the balance I sought. I needed the balance to keep it together. Any spouse experiencing the travesty of losing their family for the first night would certainly understand something has to balance life. I needed a fix of something. Sylvia and the kids left, and Rick arrived. He was a welcomed sight. My Dyna Glide was so beautiful. It needed to be ridden. I wanted to ride it. I needed to be distracted.

Rick took the first ride down the block by himself, as he wanted to get a feel for the bike. He agreed to take me for a ride, with me riding bitch. "Bitch" was the term for someone riding on the back. As a whole, male bikers don't want to be seen riding bitch. Bikers have a fairly straightforward code. While it is perfectly acceptable for a woman to ride her own bike, and it is all right for a woman to ride on the back seat, it's not acceptable for two men to ride together, with one riding on the back seat. To this day, I haven't figured out if it is all right for a male to ride behind a female. I didn't care. I needed to learn, and Rick was accommodating.

After our first ride down my isolated street, it was my turn. I lived on a desolate dead-end road, with very little traffic. Rick suggested I just practice letting out the clutch and easing into first gear, then return home. As a teacher, I had also learned to be a good student. I did as I was instructed and returned home. The next step would be a big one. I had to get up some speed and try shifting it into second gear. I again followed my master's instructions and succeeded. After several iterations up and down the street, I eventually built up the courage to make it up to third as the sun was beginning to set. It was time to call it a night.

Fortunately, I'd had enough cocktails to forget about my first night that I was sentenced into exile following my maiden voyage. I missed my kids, and my feelings of anger were already starting to build toward Sylvia. At the time, I really didn't feel like I would miss Sylvia. Besides, in the morning, I could get up and practice my lessons again without having to negotiate my own time. The time would be all mine until the kids were returned in a week. Maybe there was a good side to our separation. I started to think: Many friends had lived through divorce, and so could I. Maybe the kids would come through it too. I was starting to accept my fate. I was starting to grow accustomed to living by the rules of fate.

When my eyes opened the next morning, my acceptance of fate started to fade. It all hit. My instinct to protect my family was irrelevant. Regardless of what I felt, I was helpless. I was out of control again. I was alone. I had no family. I had no past, no future, and my present felt empty. *Why? Please forgive me. What did I do to deserve this?* Yes, I knew I still had a good life. I had no right to feel sorry for myself. Besides that, I was adopted. Didn't I understand I should be grateful? I still felt empty. I still felt alone. But maybe I had a new companion. I thought back to the exhilaration I felt the night before riding my Dyna Glide. Maybe she could pull me out of this slump. I felt alive on her. Was I looking for a material solution to my emotional problem? I didn't think so. I just needed a fix.

The sun started to filter into the room from an eastern window in my bedroom. I knew I was now street legal. The rules of the learner's permit were straightforward. I was allowed to ride only during daylight, only with a helmet, and with no passengers. I understood them, and I agreed with them. I made it down to the kitchen and brewed a stiff pot of coffee. Slowly but surely I was waking up, but I realized I had a little too much to drink the night before. I was hungover. What the hell—a couple of cups of coffee and a little time would make me feel much better. I even invested in one of the remaining bagels in the house to give my stomach something to hold on to. It was about five thirty, and I rationalized I was good enough to give it a try. If she did for me today what she had done for me last night, I should be good for the day. I was already feeling the Dyna had been a good investment. I was right. She would bring the balance I needed.

As I made it out to the garage and thought about what Rick taught me, I was already starting to get back my grip. I could do it. The choke was out, and I pressed on the starter. God, life is good. As the gasoline brought the powerful V-twin to life, it also brought back the life into my veins. I was pumped.

The road I lived on had a dogleg midway before it ended into a T intersection. As I made it from first into second, my mind was racing. I was at the edge; adrenaline and gasoline pumped through my veins. This was way too cool. I loved life. I started to drift back to college, where my good friend Fackler had a Harley. It always seemed to be a girl magnet for him. Maybe that's what I was after. My woman had left me. Was I just after something to bring another female? The dogleg had passed, and I made it through. Soon the T was coming where I had to turn around. I down shifted back into first. Mission accomplished. Rick had taught me well. I stopped at the T. I was ready for the U-turn. I let out the clutch and gave it a little gas as I started to lean into the U. Before I knew it the blacktop was turning into gravel on the far side of the T, and I panicked. The throttle and brake are both on the right. The clutch is on the left. As my right hand reached for the brake, I accidentally gave it more gas. It sent me wider into the turn and deep into a five-foot gully. I dumped the bike. My helmet hit the pavement and deeply scraped its entire left side. I should have learned from the lesson. Despite my bulky 220-pound frame, there was no way I was going to pull the bike out of the gully by myself. I was stuck. *Fuck!*

My dream was shattered. Or was it? I was in the ditch. I dumped my bike. I wasn't a biker. Or was I? Part of learning is failure, and I had failed. Or had I? I failed in mastering the bike, but had I failed in life? It was all in the mix. I was still hungover. How would I get the bike out of the ditch? I had faced bigger challenges in life before; I could overcome this shortfall. Or could I? At that moment, I wasn't sure.

Slowly, the rest of the world was coming to life. Now not only did I have to face the defeat of a failed marriage but also the failure of ditching my future life. I had placed a wager on the bike and lost. Once again

I felt like I had lost my past, my present, and now my dreamed future. I was determined not to let it get the best of me. I had to rise above my current failures. I had to rise against my past. Most of my neighbors on my block were retirees from Illinois. If I couldn't get the bike out of the ditch, how was I going to solicit one of them to help me? Most of them were at least seventy and going on their third hip replacement. All I knew was, I couldn't call Sylvia. I couldn't lower myself to that level. Fortunately, Suzzie happened to be running by.

A LITTLE HELP FROM SOME FRIENDS

Suzzie was a Schmidt. They could do anything. Even besides being a Schmidt, Suzzie could do anything. She was training for the Boston Marathon and eventually made it. Suzzie was originally a Highland, a forceful competitive family in their own right. But she added cream to the equation by marrying Matt Schmidt. Even though they weren't an old family from the area, Matt's father moved from a community slightly farther north to start a business in the graining industry. Schmidt's had owned the grain business in Belgium. But like too many other businesses in Belgium, it eventually failed. Fortunately for Matt and the rest of the family, they managed to save most of the assets before the business technically dissolved. Southeastern Wisconsin is full of very rich farmland. Schmidt's owned a lot of land. Not only was it good farmland but it was also in the path of Milwaukee metro development. Despite the failure of the grain business, they held a gold mine in land.

Belgium has an interesting history. There were reasons its name was the second half of the Cedar Grove-Belgium School District despite its larger size. Originally it had its own school district, but financially it failed and had to merge with the Cedar Grove district. Perhaps the greatest telltale clue to Belgium's future was the way it acquired its name. It was actually settled by Luxembourgers, but when they applied for their town charter the State of Wisconsin mixed up their application with the people from

Belgium who coincidentally applied for their town charter at the same time. As a result, the people from Luxembourg ended up with the name Belgium, and the people from Belgium ended up with the name Luxembourg. Neither community did anything about the mix up. They simply accepted fate. I'm not sure what the implications of me eventually settling there are.

I originally met Suzzie through her sister-in-law Martha. Martha was married to Matt's brother John. Martha was an English teacher in my school district. At the end of my first year of teaching, Martha held an annual end of the year party. Besides, Martha lived in a beautiful house not far from ours, on the shores of Lake Michigan. Martha was one of the first teachers in the district I got to know well. Besides the commonality of living on the beach, we, as well as John, graduated from University of Wisconsin-Stout. It allowed us to share a common bond. It was through the party I met Matt and Suzzie. Martha, John, Matt, and Suzzie became some of our closest friends in the neighborhood. They helped us learn the vernacular nuances of the region. They were also among the first I had shared my adoption discovery with. Besides, Matt was one of the first I told of my impending divorce. Matt and I commiserated over a six pack in his back forty.

Suzzie was on the last leg of one of her fifteen-mile training circuits. Fortunately for me, Suzzie happened to be running by and was able to help me out of the ditch. The bike wasn't fatally damaged, so I was able to ride it home and lick my wounds. I knew I had to get back on the horse, or I would never get back on it again. I did. The taillight was busted off, but its engine roared back to life once I commanded. It was a painful, but necessary ride home. It was such a metaphor for the rest of my life at the time. So many parts of my life seemed busted. The rest of the week was spent taking turns between accomplishing house projects to get it ready for the market, taking practice rides up and down my street on the bike, and venturing out during the evening hours. I started visiting the local watering holes.

Soon it was my turn to have the kids for the week. We had agreed to complete the trade-off on Sunday mornings, and as I called them a few times during the week, I was familiar to the specifics of what they had done. I had made it through the first week alone but was looking forward to seeing them again. They were happy to return home. Sylvia had a two-bedroom apartment, so all three of them shared a room. In our home on the lake, the girls shared a room, while Tony had his own. I was also the keeper of the family critters. We had Luke the dog, and a rabbit named Bitsy. They were excited to see their pets.

During that first week by myself, I must have completed hundreds of trips up and down our street. I had duct taped the busted turn signal in place, and fortunately for me it still worked. As far as I could tell, besides the dings in the gas tank and some minor scratches, the light was the only significant damage. Eventually, the shifting pattern became more natural, and I got a sense for the clutch and throttle. Even though I was feeling good about my progress, I still recognized it would be best for me to take the motorcycle training class. I signed up at the local technical college for a class in mid-July. It was the first available opening.

The kids were all attending summer school, so I had the mornings to myself. I tried to complete my self-inflicted goals in the morning and be able to do activities with them in the afternoons. That often included working on the house for a while and getting in some practice time on the bike before I had to pick them up. I was thankful we had enrolled them in summer school in that during the week together it gave me a bit of a breather to do the shopping, clean the house, get the laundry done, and complete all the tasks delegated to a single parent. During our first week together, I was conservative about what challenges I would venture on the bike. Basically, I stuck to the familiar routine of riding up and down the street. I also managed to buy a new taillight at the local dealer and get it attached to the bike. It was a small accomplishment, but it felt good.

On the other hand, I was not satisfied with progress on completion of the garage. Suddenly the task seemed overwhelming. This was new to me. I had long ago assumed an identity of a self-sufficient man, a one-man island in a way. I believed if I put my mind to it, I could accomplish anything. But this was, of course, before I found out I was a bastard. Something had changed; that feeling was gone. I just couldn't do it anymore. I had contacted my Realtor about selling the house, and we both agreed the garage should be fairly complete, and a few other repair projects completed on the house prior to putting it on the market. I contacted a local contractor, and we came up with a plan. I would complete the bottom part of the garage, and he would complete the top. Given the upcoming sale of the house, I thought we would be able to afford it. I asked Sylvia about my plan, and she concurred.

Sylvia still controlled me. It was the fate I accepted. Once again the role of the adoptee kicked into full gear. Even though Sylvia laid the groundwork of an impending divorce, I was still submissive. Most would have moved into the anger phase, yet I continued to beg for her forgiveness, despite from my perspective that I had done nothing wrong. Adoptees, and especially late-discovery adoptees, are notorious for being "pleasers." Some of the books I had read indicated it was the result of the "primal wound." Primal wound was the psychological scar that came from being abandoned at birth. Whether I suffered from primal wound or not didn't really matter. All I knew was I had to try to please. That didn't necessarily mean I accomplished my goal—all it meant was I was destined to believe I was a subordinate to everybody and everything around me. Obviously, based on the fate of my marriage, I didn't succeed. At the time I was more than willing to accept the fact the wrap-up of our uncompleted home was my responsibility. I was the one who had to wrap up the uncompleted ends.

At first the new routine seemed awkward, but eventually I grew accustomed to the split family way of life. In between my weeks with the kids, I practiced my rides on my Dyna. Each week was one to look forward to. One week I was with my kids, and the next I was able to practice my bike-riding skills. Getting the house market ready was work and not anything to look forward to. It was no longer our home nor my future. Initially, it was difficult receiving the children and seeing Sylvia as it brought back the disintegration of my family. I felt bad for what Sylvia and I were doing to the kids and that they would have to live in a split family. Like internalizing adoption, I was starting to internalize my family's destruction. But as someone who had adapted to many new routines, I also began to settle into the role of our family as that of a split family.

TRYING NEW IDENTITIES

Following Sylvia's physical departure, our counseling sessions were moved to every two to three weeks. The crisis wasn't averted, and the counselor indicated the insurance would only cover visits every two weeks. We had to make due. While the sessions didn't meet the original goal of keeping us intact, they did seem to produce another desirable result. In retrospect, I believe they helped keep a lid on a potentially explosive situation. Each of us, were able to remain fairly civil as we tackled each of our new frontiers. The kids were experiencing a somewhat child centered split, which I think helped minimize its negative impacts on all of them. Additionally, for both Sylvia and I, the diminished anger level allowed each of us to grow in our own ways, which was needed at the time. Dr. Trott had divided us into a split counseling routine. Instead of meeting together we met separately and worked on our own individual issues. My plan was one of exploring my anger and how I directed it.

In the meantime, my practice time on my bike was that of an altered state. It was a time when everything else was out of my mind, and I only focused on the mechanics of riding a motorcycle. My near death experiences seemed to come less frequent, but often enough to keep my attention. To some extent, gut wrenching fear blocked out everything else from my mind. I didn't feel adopted. I didn't feel split. I didn't feel abandoned. All I felt was survival. It was wonderful.

I started to learn a new way to live. In a way, I started to live a second adolescence. I was suddenly free of the responsibilities of a married family man and could start to live my own life as an independent person. Day by day I started to forge a new independence. Eventually, I was confident enough to make it beyond my own half-mile dead-end street. I started with a turn to the right at the T. Next I was able to make it around a country mile. First, second, and third gear started to feel comfortable. It started to feel as comfortable as my new identity as a single parent. I moved beyond the state of terror on the bike and eventually started to actually enjoy the exhilaration of riding a motorcycle. The feeling went from burden to reward. I started to love my Dyna Glide. It became a place to be me; it became a new foundation.

In late June, it was finally time to take my motorcycle class. I had already felt comfortable enough to make the thirty-mile country route to Lake Shore Technical College (LTC), where the class was offered, on the Dyna. The quickest and most direct route was on Interstate I-43, but I preferred a back roads rural route. Even though the interstate was remote between Cedar Grove and LTC, I still was less comfortable traveling by and around semitrucks. I found the wind currents around semis are unnerving. I also found I could take the country roads at my own pace, and they were much more scenic.

The class was offered over a weekend. Bookwork was completed in one four-hour session on Friday night, followed by a Saturday and Sunday consumed with two eight-hour riding sessions. The last two hours of the Sunday session contained a final road test, which satisfied the state's regular license requirement. Sylvia agreed to swap some time with the kids so I could complete the course without having to arrange for a babysitter. I was appreciative. As the weekend came and went, I found I learned much about what I was doing right, and what I needed to relearn. By Sunday evening, I was riding home with my regular motorcycle license. It felt like another accomplishment in my life. Although I was still a "newbie" in the motorcycle world, I felt one step closer to the identity of a biker.

I had reestablished frequent contact with my old friend Sean from Washington, DC, once Sylvia broke her news. Sean had been through a divorce, and his was a very anger-filled divorce. Sean offered support and allowed for a healthy dose of venting on my part. Sean had two children, Megan and Connor, who were several years older than mine. After several discussions Sean offered to come to visit with his kids for a long weekend at the end of the summer. I gladly accepted his offer. Sean and I had known each other for nearly twenty years. We met when I worked in Rockford, Illinois, which was where I also met Sylvia. They were perhaps the two most important relationships I had acquired in my life, and they both came from a place I loathed. In retrospect, Rockford really wasn't that bad of a place, but for a young, single, unmarried working professional, it offered little opportunity for a social life. Rockford seemed to be capital of the Rust Belt in the early 1980s. It earned the lowest ranking, very bottom, of the places rated almanac during the second year I lived there. My only comfort at the time was its proximity to my hometown, Milwaukee. It was an easy ninety-minute ride on a sparsely traveled interstate. I spent most weekends in Milwaukee during my time in Rockford.

Sean was a mechanical engineer at the Byron nuclear plant, which was under construction near Rockford. He grew up in a large Irish Catholic family in the seaside community of Tom's River, New Jersey. Sean's girlfriend Kelly, soon-to-be wife, moved with Sean into my apartment building. She was an aggressive paralegal with aspirations to attend law school. I dated one of Kelly's friends for a while, which seemed to get my friendship with Sean off to a start. Once we discovered our mutual attraction for dark beer and the nighttime activities of the local pub scene, our friendship seemed to grow. Eventually, Sean and I expanded our relationship beyond beer and found the competition of racquetball and running invigorating, to say the least. Sean and Kelly moved to Washington, DC, when Kelly got accepted at George Washington Law School. Sean escaped Rockford six months before I managed to move to California. Years later while in architecture school, I took a summer job in Washington, DC, and Sean indicated I could rent a spare room in their house. During that summer we enjoyed much dark beer together.

Sean, Megan, and Connor came to the lake house for their visit. We had a great time enjoying moonlit campfires on the beach, kayaking, and playing in the waves. His visit helped me settle into my newly perceived identity as a divorcée. As I saw him and his children interact in a loving and natural way, I was able to imagine my relationship with my children taking a similar course. I now started to believe there was life after divorce. It was amazing how many things had changed in the last several years. Considering how attached I was to being a natural offspring in an intact family, my new identity as an adoptee, in a split family was starting to feel less awkward, and almost comfortable. My newfound comfort level also seemed to reinvigorate my drained batteries. I felt a new surge of energy to complete the painting and finish work on the house, so it could be sold, and I could move on with my life.

The kids seemed to be adjusting to their new way of life. Sylvia also seemed to be moving forward. She was no longer depressed and indicated she was sleeping better. I oscillated between periods of peace and despair. While I had the kids, I found activities that would make us all happy. Some days were spent at the zoo, while others were spent at the beach. My goal was to make them happy. When I was away from the kids, I spent endless hours exploring back roads and started to venture out farther in the beautiful Wisconsin rural countryside. On the other hand, I periodically found myself depressed. I knew I had a good life, and experienced true moments of happiness, but something was still troubling me. It was beyond my feelings of loneliness when I wasn't with my kids; it was something deeper. I started to think about the adoption issues again and wanted to resolve my search. I had let it rest for quite a while, but most aspects of where I left off were still fresh in my mind. I had to resume my search for Don's brother, Ron. I had to find out whatever became of Don, and if there were any more siblings. Something pushed me to go further. Periodically, I completed internet searches for Ron, which inevitably led to an endless string of dead-end calls. But at least now I had something to take me away from my self-inflicted torture. I could always hop on the bike, and within ten miles, my mind would be over one million miles away.

As midsummer approached, I decided to take a sixty-mile ride to the Harley dealer in Fond du Lac, Wisconsin. Riding to Harley dealerships became a way to explore new regions on the bike. Inevitably, I would return home with a souvenir, such as a shirt, a shot glass, or some other overpriced trinket from my destination. I took a fairly straightforward route to Fond du Lac, on a very straight, bumpy, and boring state highway.

Highway 23 was a direct route from Sheboygan to Fond du Lac, but it was heavily traveled and in bad need of repair. Eventually, I found myself in Fond du Lac and came upon Bob's Harley-Davidson. After my visit I decided to find a more scenic and hopefully more enjoyable route home. I examined the map and decided on Highway 41. It would land me just west of home, but I was certain I could find a county highway to get me home.

As I started out, I realized I had made the right decision. The winding roads led past a variety of cattle and horse farms, with many curves and hills that allowed me to get a feel for what biking was all about. Eventually, it straightened out, and I realized it was about time to start cutting east on back roads. When I looked over to the east, I could see the distant Kettles. The Kettles, actually known as the Kettle Moraines, are the remnants of the glaciers that once covered most of Wisconsin. As the glaciers melted and started their retreat north, they left a series of deposits known as the Moraines, which are high conelike hills and ridges. In addition, they left smaller glacial lakes, which are the Kettles. It's a particularly beautiful area in Wisconsin, which is cut by winding roads with sharp inclines, followed by breathtaking declines. I scoured my map and noticed County Highway F, which curved through a town called Dundee. I knew the road and the town from previous camping trips with Jim and Sam. It was a scenic area and included many twisting roads around Long Lake State Park. When camping, I remembered hearing the distant thunder of motorcycles on the other side of Long Lake as we lounged on the camp beach, watching our kids swim in the lake. Jim always indicated it was the bikers in Dundee. At that point I knew it was worth investigating. I took a left onto Highway F and let the open road be my guide.

Something in me started to understand. It was more than the simple understanding of how the mechanics of operating the bike that captured biking enthusiasts. And it was more than an image or longing to be something else besides the one in the minivan. It had to do with the feel of the road beneath my feet as the bike ate every corner. It was a connection of rubber to the road, a connection of the soul to life, and a feeling of being totally alive. I felt one with the bike and one with the road. As the trail grew more challenging, however, and I began to wind through the Kettles, my stomach started to match the growling of my V-twin. I realized I needed to stop for a bite to eat. The Road House seemed like the perfect venue. Approaching from the west, I couldn't help but noticing the wafting smell of fresh fried grease, with an aromatic hint of beef. Even its appearance seemed to cry Harley. A two-story gray pool hall, it reeked of too many renovations since its apparent early 1900s inception. It wanted me to stop. I followed its command.

The over-the-top, smoke-filled stench hit me like a ton of bricks, but I didn't mind. It felt real. Bev was behind the bar. She was a biker. I could tell. I took a seat at the bar and asked for a menu. Bev accommodated my request. The lunch crowd was in full force. It was obviously a popular local crowd, full of many laborers. One predictable aspect of rural Wisconsin was you won't find many stuffy tie types. There are no tall glass office towers filled with businesses and people trying to look busy. The economy just doesn't provide for that kind of luxury. Everyone has a very real and purposeful job to do in the community, whether it's being a carpenter, farmer, mechanic, or truck driver. Every job is easily definable and real. The Road House was full of real people. Most of the crowd appeared to have many more miles under their skin than their age would suggest. These were high-mileage people.

I ordered the Road House bucket. It was basically a mushroom and Swiss burger with fries, along with a Miller High Life. I had already learned you were either a Miller or a Bud person in rural Wisconsin. Given my uncle Les, I wasn't about to order a Bud. As I enjoyed my burger, I looked around and observed the crowd. Bev seemed to take notice to me and began to strike up a conversation. I wasn't a local or a regular, so I'm sure her curiosity got the best of her. Who was this fresh piece of meat with an obviously new Harley shirt on? What was I doing in this neck of the woods? The natives seemed curious. Fortunately, I was sizable enough to not be too afraid. Rural Wisconsin boys are big boys, but I figured I was big enough to fit in. Bev was interesting in that she appeared to be a pure biker type, complete with a voice that screamed way too many Camel Straights. But at the same time she seemed to exhibit an insightfulness that was beyond her initial appearance.

As we talked, a commonality surfaced: she was from Rockford, Illinois. This was the same place I met my best friend and my wife. Dundee seemed to be my *Twilight Zone*. It seemed to be a place where many aspects of my life came together. Before I finished my burger, beer, and headed home, Bev suggested I stop by Sunday afternoon. The Road House had an open jam with a band that attracted many bikers from all walks of life, and she thought I would like it. I agreed and headed out. During the ride home, I realized my Dyna was starting to feel like home. I now knew I was starting to formulate a new identity.

As I wound myself around the twisting roads of the Kettles and eventually onto the straights that would lead me east to my home, I couldn't help but reflect on the last few years. So many changes had occurred. But life seemed amazing, and I was living a very full life. As I reflected, watching the sun set on my back, I thought of many of the events that fate seemed to be using to push my life in different directions. Witnessing my parents' death was a lifetime experience some people see, and I was glad I hadn't missed. Although it was hard, I thanked God I was there. I didn't know how I would have lived with myself had I not been.

But I wished I could have shared my discovery with them. My late discovery was unique to me, and not many had ventured down that road. It wasn't so much that it was awful being adopted; it was more finding out later in life, and then realizing the legal restrictions that came with the label. After all, I was an Eagle Scout, someone who believed in the system and then I found out the system had lied to me, about me. But it wasn't until I found out my birth status that I realized I had so many less rights to my identity.

I even felt thankful for the near loss of my daughter Grace. Painful as it was, it gave me a fuller appreciation of my family. Thank God for the bike. Thank God for Nic and Chic. Thank God for Sylvia's gift of children. At that point I couldn't say thank God for Sylvia. I still had some anger issues.

That weekend I took Bev up on her invite and made it to the Road

House for the open jam. As I approached on my bike, I was amazed at the magnitude of chrome and exotic paint jobs that lined the street. I had never seen so many motorcycles in one place in my life. The band was the Mark Pinier Band, and they played the type of hard-rocking blues I expected to hear in a biker bar. The place was packed. I was in awe. A dense haze of green-and-blue smoke filled the air, and the music was barely understandable over the roar of the loud gregarious crowd packed from wall to wall. While I didn't feel nervous, I would definitely say I was in an alert state.

As I made my way to get a Miller, I heard someone call my name. *How could this be?* I was sure I wouldn't know anybody here. The voice didn't sound familiar, so I knew it wasn't Bev. As I looked behind the bar, a familiar face greeted me, and asked what I wanted. It was one of the school's lunch ladies, Sonya. I couldn't believe my eyes. There was actually a familiar face in this gnarly crowd. Her shift would soon be over, and she wanted me to meet her husband, Ollie.

As I outlined my story, first with my marriage separation, followed by my birth status oddity, Ollie seemed to feel I was genuine and not playing any games. At that point I was ecstatic to find so many people who seemed to share my newly found religion of the open road. Ollie represented the ultimate biker and was like a complete set of the biker encyclopedias. He had been on the road many years and had millions of miles under his boots. Dressed in colors, Ollie was a Union Rider. Union Riders were a local affiliation of a national club. Colors refer to the patches sewed on the vests and jackets that depict which club the bikers rode with. As our discussion continued, I found my attention being sucked into a whole new world. My insatiable appetite for knowledge about this world fueled my curiosity. Like a moth drawn to a flame, I found I couldn't take my eyes off the potentially fatal flame that lay ahead. This was the world of bad boys and biker babes. Ollie was like a social vortex. I was in awe.

During the Fourth of July, Sylvia took the kids for her annual trek to Pennsylvania. It was the first family vacation without me, as she decided to take them to the ocean in New Jersey, which would be their first time experiencing the ocean. I was mortified. I hadn't yet quite gotten the concept of divorce. It meant I wouldn't be there for the kids every first. I told her of my feelings, but at that point hurt seemed to be the point. The more I pleaded with her to see if there would be a future time we could do it together, the more she seemed determined to make the event hers. I was starting to understand. I realized it would be a very hard Fourth of July. I decided to lick my wounds by attending a friend's Fourth of July party in Cedarburg at a park on the Milwaukee River.

Cedarburg is a quaint turn of the century town, filled with a cream city brick and cobble stone shopping district. It also happens to be in the path of the expensive Milwaukee home swath, so it's fairly up scale. Of course I took my bike. Many old friends were there, most of which Sylvia wasn't thrilled with. Bill was there.

When we got married, I had many friends, which centered around Hap. Hap, Harlen Carlson, and I graduated from high school together. My class had 444 students, so, of course, I didn't know all of them. I was aware of Hap—after all, he was in the popular crowd, which I was not. Hap was not really aware of me, which was evident when I ran into Hap in Rockford. As fate would have it, both Hap and I ended up in Rockford, Illinois, after college. I was working at one of the local hospitals, and Hap was an assistant manager at the mall. After a long Friday, one of the few I had stayed in Rockford, I went to Stash O'Niels. There, huddled over the free peanuts at the bar, was Hap. Elated to see a familiar face, I quickly approached Hap and introduced myself. He hadn't a clue who I was. But he, too, was a newcomer to Rockford and more than willing to expand his social circles. Hap didn't need to expand his social circles in that he was a social conduit. He knew everyone. He was easily one of the six degrees of separation away from Princess Diana. After a night of many beers and some conversation, I had fallen into Hap's social circles. One of Hap's friends was Bill, who grew up with Eric, who was Hap's roommate in college.

While Bill and I had been mutual friends of friends, neither of us understood the turns our distant friendship was about to take. Bill noticed my bike. A fetish Bill had acquired after his recent divorce was a taste for motorcycles. Bill was a Honda guy, the other *H*. He noticed my bike and immediately started a conversation, which led to many bike rides that summer. By the end of summer, Bill had become a regular at the Road House and many of my other stops on the way. Bill became one of my strongest supports as I grappled with the concepts of what divorce and family were all about. At the same time, I became one of Bill's strongest entrees into what the social side of biking was all about. I had already gotten to know many people, and this time I was the social conduit.

Once I felt comfortable with a passenger, I tried to lure Sylvia into my newfound discovery. After all, since she didn't like who I was before, maybe she would like who I'd become. It was worth a try. Initially, I asked her if she'd like to take a ride up to a remote little beach I'd found north of Sheboygan called Pico Bay. To me, once again it was similar to our honeymoon location. But she didn't feel comfortable on the back of my bike. It just didn't feel safe. So I thought I would try something a little less threatening. How about a two-mile ride up Sauk Trail to the local beach for a lunch? She agreed to give it a try. I packed a lunch, complete with a bottle of wine, and arranged for a sitter. I was still oscillating between hating her and loving her. I had a lot to learn. We hopped on the bike and made the trip up to the beach. Sylvia seemed all right, but just a little tense. Despite the fact the lunch went fairly well, I could tell she was nervous about the ride home. I was right. By the time we made it back, she was a nervous wreck. She tried to hide it, but I could tell she didn't enjoy the experience. While I was high on the trip, she was definitely low. I realized I was the only one who enjoyed my newfound identity. I didn't take it well.

LIFE ON THE ROAD
(August 2003)

My summer was fading, and so was any hope of reconciliation. It wasn't going to happen. I had to move on. Luckily, I had some tools. Isn't that what shop teachers are supposed to be good at? Shop teachers are good with tools, and my bike was now a social tool. I could further explore the world of biking without a guilty conscious. Sure, I had kids and a wife, but it wasn't my choice to split. I decided to take advantage of my newly found freedom. Why not explore a new world? I knew I wasn't who I thought I was, so I became open to finding out who this bastard really was. I was the definition of a bastard, wasn't I? Sure, I would deal with my duties as a teacher and a father. But during my free time, I needed to find out who this asshole child really was. Don abandoned his duties, and I was still going to keep my financial and parental responsibilities, so why couldn't I really dive into the world of biking and see where it could take me? Life was too short not to have fun! I had been prepped. I was ready for the procedure.

The more I went out, the more my social life expanded. Once I entered Ollie's social vortex, everything, and everyone became a blur. He knew everyone on the road. It was phenomenal. Everyone I met led to dozens of more friendships. Once accepted into the world of biking, the brotherhood became an endless voyage. Somehow I did the right thing at the right time. Or, maybe, I was just one of them; I was another lost soul in the hurricane of life. I was never pretentious and always honest; I was who I was and it wasn't pretty. I was un-forgiven too. I migrated back to angry man music. It seemed to suit me well. When I didn't have the kids, the Road House became a regular trip. Soon I became a familiar face, and I met everyone else who made the Road House a regular stop. I was now starting to discover the social aspects of having a bike. It felt like a good discovery.

One hot summer day, I was on my way back from a ride in the Kettles. While heading past a town about fifteen miles west of my home, Random Lake, I felt something fall off my motorcycle. I was traveling about fifty miles per hour at the time, and the bike continued to run, so I didn't feel it was critical. I was wrong. As I proceeded into my stopping routine, I suddenly noticed I no longer had a shifter pedal. I was in fourth gear. This was definitely a problem. I could always clutch it to a stop, but without a shifter I knew I couldn't really get going again.

After I brought the bike to a halt, I walked back and retrieved it. While I could place it on the sprocket, there was no way to tighten it, and keep it in place while I completed my trip home. Fortunately, I knew of a biker bar in Random; surely someone there must have a wrench. My gamble paid off. Sparky was at the bar and overheard me talking to Kimmy, the bartender. Sparky was a Rite-A-Way. Right-A-Ways were a local club without a national affiliation. An older club, Right-A-Ways had long ago earned the respect of the other clubs, and Sparky was a well-respected member within the Rite-A-Ways. After we attached my shifter, I repaid Sparky with a few longnecks, and we exchanged stories and numbers before I headed home. It was the start of a good friendship. As our social engagements became more periodic, I became much more acquainted with his philosophies regarding fate.

Another good friend I met on the road was Rich, who had also recently become divorced and bought his bike as a balancing tool. Riding had long been part of his life on the farm where he grew up. But it wasn't until his wife left that he decided to make biking a way of life and not just an entertainment. As Rich and I talked more, we discovered we had another mutual interest, snowmobiling. We decided when the snow flew; he would show me the trails in the area. Rich introduced me to A Brotherhood Against Totalitarian Enactments (ABATE).

In the seemingly rambling ways of bikers, the clubs and organizations had a fundamental structure. Somewhere between meetings and organized rides for charities, bikers sought structure like everyone else. ABATE was a biking organization. While it was originally started as an antihelmet law movement, its fundamental premise was that government shouldn't create laws that restricted an individual's right to pursue happiness. It meant people should be free to live their life as they needed, as long as it wasn't infringing on the rights of others. While I didn't feel I was ready to commit to joining a club, ABATE seemed loose enough, and I did believe in its fundamental premise. I had already realized the government controlled too many aspects of my life—namely, my identity.

Whether I chose to ride with a helmet or not wasn't as much of an issue as was the thought of making the government less intrusive.

At the end of August, Harley-Davidson held its hundredth-year anniversary party in Milwaukee. Given my newbiness and the associated hype, I recognized I was definitely part of the hype. Even though I was aware that Sylvia was most likely not part of the hype, I decided to try to bring her into the fold by inviting her to the culminating event in downtown Milwaukee. It was a risk, but I decided I wanted to give it a try. Earlier in the celebration summer, I had taken a few rides down to Brady Street on Milwaukee's eastside. Each event attended brought back an invigorating spirit of youth that I thought might infuse romantic feelings within Sylvia. Reluctantly she decided to give it a try. While I wouldn't say the event wooed her over, it definitely brought her closer to my world than my attempt at Amsterdam Beach.

SHIFTING INTO FINAL GEAR

At last, after months of getting prepared, the house was put on the market. Although I wasn't sure if it was the right thing to do, I knew it had to be done. Sylvia had indicated I could keep the house, and she would take the proceeds from selling the cabin up north. Financially, that would be roughly equal to me keeping my inheritance and splitting the net equity we made during our marriage. But between the remaining mortgage on the house and the high property taxes, I knew I couldn't afford to stay there long. Neither of us had filed for divorce, but it didn't seem like we were any closer to reconciliation. We were in a bit of a stalemate. I also realized it might take some time to sell the house, given its price. Our price was in the range of similar houses in the local market, but its unique floor plan and design would require a specific type of buyer. Besides, the holiday season was rapidly approaching, and we knew once Thanksgiving came the market would die off until the following spring.

I had put our house on the market, but my plan had no purpose. Most people sell their homes knowing where they will move. For me, it had become a move out of necessity, not desire. I didn't know where I would go. But at the same time I didn't care. I had found a new world of defining homes without a place. So many people I ran with had no permanent structure that defined home. Home was somewhere they defined by the moment. I was starting to define myself by the moment, not the place. Perhaps it had to do with my newfound belief of family. Certainly I was struggling with what family was, and where it existed. I definitely didn't have the answer.

The school year started, and I found I needed more. Once again I was open with my students; I was going through a divorce and exploring the world of an angry man. Somehow this seemed to reach a new level of connection with my tech ed. kids. Many of them were angry from the assortment of blows life had dealt them. Split families, alcoholic parents, drug-addicted parents—they all seemed to have a connection. My new nickname given to me by my students was Hardcore. My content hadn't changed, but my attitude had. Even though I tried to keep the same demeanor, I wasn't the same person I was before. As I explored my newfound social outlet, I actually met many of their parents on the road. Their parents seemed to be recharged by the prospect that one of their own actually made it into the hallowed halls of education. They may have fucked up in life, but that didn't mean they were worthless. That didn't mean their children were worthless. They wanted a future for their children; they desperately wanted to have someone see value in their children. I saw value in their children. I was one of them. It was a new chapter in my education, in education. Every kid has value.

As the school year progressed, my colleges saw a difference. Their most insightful comment in the lunchroom was I seemed happier. I don't know that I was actually happier. To me, it seemed like I was just freer to be me. I started to realize I had been tightly wrapped up in an identity that strangled me from myself. Whether it was an identity of someone deprived of his or her biological roots or an identity of someone in a broken marriage, I wasn't sure. Maybe it was a little of both. I was finally free to express my own unique expression of life. It felt good to express my life.

Weeks with my kids were hard and joy filled at the same time. When they were with me, I tried to appreciate them more. I tried and had to be more involved with their day-to-day lives. But between making supper, doing dishes, cleaning the house, and carting them between their various activities, there was little room for anything beyond the necessities. Times to relax and take a breath seemed far and few between. When I didn't have them, life was the opposite. Every night was a new venture on my bike. I had learned the biking circuit and began to have regular routes with periodic watering holes on the way as I found new social exploration spots. I was no longer just a local at the Road House, but I was also getting to be a regular at many places on the way to the Road House. I was starting to think; my new life wasn't really all that bad. I was starting to feel comfortable living my newfound life.

Frost on the road in the early morning brought about other changes. I beefed up my riding wardrobe to prolong the biking season. I knew the Dyna didn't run well when the temperature fell below forty degrees, so I was soon anticipating putting the bike away for the winter. Fortunately, we had a warm fall, and I was able to take the bike to school when I didn't have the kids and on many of the weekends. The kids at school seemed to like when I brought the bike in. In between counseling sessions, Sylvia and I tried to occasionally spend time together. I was still taking firefighting classes and attending monthly practices at the firehouse. My life was feeling full. Yet I still found myself bouncing in and out of Abandon Land.

Another holiday season was on its way. My familiar visit to the memories of Nic reappeared, but this time I tried to focus on his life, not his dying days. He had spent most of my adolescence and his later life in the basement working on wood projects. Over the course of his lifetime, he had developed an expertise at shaping wood into both useful and artistic expressions. After my mother's death, I acquired most of his projects. Among the two grandfather clocks, spinning wheel, benches, tables, and various other masterpieces was a legacy to behold. One piece, a revolving bookcase was made toward the later years. To my surprise, Sylvia appeared one day and indicated it was hers. My bitterness was enraged at the audacity of her demand. She further explained that engraved on the bottom was a message indicating he had made it for her. Even if he made it for her, to me it was in the context of her being my wife. Certainly he would not want her to have it after she did *this*. After a cooling-down period, I proceeded to empty its contents and check the bottom. Sure enough, there engraved on the bottom along with the year he made it, his name, and Wauwatosa, Wisconsin, were the words "To Sylvia." I was mortified. She didn't push the issue, and I never confessed my investigations.

The betrayal of my father seemed to coincide with the betrayal of many of the other extended family members of my adoptive family. Once Sylvia had left, I noticed a peculiar trend. They frequently socialized with her, and seldom with me. When I would get the kids back, after their week away, I would often ask them what they did during the week. Even though I was familiar with most of their activities, there was periodically a "We went to your aunt's and uncle's for dinner on Thursday." At first I thought it was nice they were continuing to include my kids in their lives. But as the incidences increased over time, it became apparent the invites only occurred when Sylvia had the kids. At one point I brought it to Sylvia's attention. She indicated she had also noticed it and really had no explanation, but was enjoying the time with them. It seemed not only would Sylvia be taking my nuclear family from me but also the fragments of what had been my extended family.

Fortunately, the winter had been mild with relatively little snow and mild temperatures. At first I was hesitant to take out the bike when it was below forty degrees in that the spark plugs would rapidly foul up, which made the bike run rough. But as I experienced the decay of my nuclear and my extended family, I progressively relied on my road family more. I had started to make good friends, who had little ties to my bastardly past and always greeted me with a friendly smile and in some cases an affectionate hug. I soon learned to carry an extra set of spark plugs and simply replaced them on the road when needed. During the holiday season of 2003, the bike wasn't the only thing running rough. It was a very dark holiday season.

CHAPTER 7

TIME TO MOVE ON
JANUARY 2004

don't know if I put the house on the market to actually sell or because I knew it was what was supposed to be done when you were getting a divorce. As I didn't have a plan as to where I would move, I really hadn't invested a lot of time into the thought of actually leaving. Suddenly that changed. My listing agent, Carol, called. She wanted me to look at something. A house about one mile from mine was about to go on the market. Carol knew I needed to move, and she thought it might be a good fit. The house itself had little to do with the equation though. It was the land she thought might be a good fit. The house came with 18.5 wooded acres with large ravines and creeks. As the house was on the eastside of Sauk Trail, it meant the zoning would make the land subdividable. Most of the surrounding land was zoned agricultural and couldn't contain more than one single-family residence per thirty-two acres. The house itself was comprised of a stone base house built in 1860 with several additions, which included ones from 1890, 1920, and 1950. Unfortunately, the house hadn't been updated much since the late 1960s. The last family who lived in the home bought it in 1947, raised their family, and lived out their final days in the home. The house was being sold as part of the estate of Mr. Kashinska, who died about one year earlier. His son currently occupied the home and would leave upon its sale. The house was to go on the market in about one week, and Carol suspected it would sell fast. As Carol lived in the area, she would have rather seen the house go to someone with a vested interest in the area as opposed to a developer who might not appreciate the beauty of the land. I initially thought the last thing I wanted was another project house. After all, I just gained my every other week of freedom, and didn't think I wanted to give it up yet. But my curiosity over ruled and I said I would take a look. I decided to look at the house when I had the kids. It was an activity we could do together, and this way I wouldn't lose any bike time. They thought it would be fun, as the home was on their school bus route and they always wondered what it was like on the inside.

It was a mid-January sunny winter day. As the son of the previous owner was the only occupant, most of the house was fairly empty. The temperature had also been turned down on the second story to reduce heating costs. There is a reason the owners always leave when Realtors show a house. When we entered, Graces first comment was "What stinks?" It was evident that the previous owners had animals. It also reflected the dark cave like atmosphere popular in the late 1960s and early 1970s. But soon the kids went off on their own tour, while Carol did her best to show me the best of the house.

It was beyond a fixer-upper. It was a bulldozer. Or was it? My initial impression was the plan was one of nodes and pathways. Long halls lead to distinctively different living spaces, a natural result of being added on to several times. While much of the wooden paneling, sculptured orange shag carpeting, and yellow Formica surfaces did their best to hide the houses historic qualities, its windows set deep into the twenty-two-inch stone walls and its massive stone fireplace suggested it was may be a diamond in the rough. Hell, it was still buried in the coal seam.

In addition to the house, an older granary, a lean-to, and a small tar-papered shack were located on the front portion of the land. The granary had a certain charm with a newer metal roof. The two other buildings looked like they were far more work than they were worth. Eventually, we started to make our way into the backwoods. As we passed through an entanglement of thickets, Grace complained that this reminded her of our cabin, and she wanted to go back to the car. Soon the underbrush gave way to a canopied forest with deep ravines and frozen creek beds. I was mesmerized. To me, the beauty was breath taking. Tony found a deer antler shed and thought it was a good omen. Maybe I did too. When we made it back to the car, I told Carol it was interesting, but I didn't think I wanted to make that big of a commitment to a house. I was fried on commitments. She saw my hesitation and indicated she would keep me posted. I indicated that would be fine.

While at work the following week, Carol called. The house had an offer within the first fifteen minutes of being on the market. She suggested I act quickly if I was at all interested. Something in me snapped. I wanted the house. But I couldn't afford the house. Was this the time to dive into something like this? I had mentioned it to Sylvia, and at this point she was fairly amenable to let me do as I saw needed. The lake house hadn't sold yet, and we didn't really have any good prospects on the table. Every couple of weeks Carol would have another showing, but to date our only offer was ridiculously low. Maybe we could get a bridge loan? We had quite a bit of equity in the house, so I thought it might be worth a try. But was this a once in a lifetime chance? I had tackled big projects before, so maybe this is what I needed to get my life back on track. I must be nuts! I called the bank. I emailed my intentions to Sylvia. I didn't want to try to make a move without her awareness. I was afraid there could be legal ramifications.

By the time I finished my call to the bank to get the paperwork for pre-approval underway, I already had another message from Carol. The owner accepted the first offer. But there was still hope. The accepted offer was from the contractor who completed the work on my house, Chris Watry. Chris was also the neighbor to the property for sale. Carol thought he planned on splitting it up and might be interested in selling off a lot. I knew Chris, as he also was the contractor who built my uncle Bob's house, which I designed. Chris indicated he was interested. His offer was a joint offer with a friend who was also going through a divorce. Chris wanted the front house for his son, and the other party wanted the back lot. It sat high on a bluff, above the shores of Lake Michigan. While it didn't have beach access, as there was a string of beach homes at the bottom of the bluff, it did offer seasonal views, and the waves of Lake Michigan were often heard.

Once again things began to change. Carol called the following week to let me know it looked like the first offer was about to fall apart. Chris's partner's divorce proceedings had taken a turn for the worse, and he wouldn't be able to ante up. I could put in a secondary offer that would allow me to catch the property once Chris's offer fell apart. I told Carol to put together the paperwork and swing by in the evening to put everything into place. By the next morning I had an accepted offer in place. It looked like I now had a place to move.

Having things fall into place seemed to act as a catalyst. I was letting go. For nine months I had desperately held on to any thread of hope for somehow figuring out how to have an intact family again. It's not that I wanted to go back to where we were, but somehow I thought it would be possible to all live together again. I knew Sylvia's feelings weren't the only ones that needed to change. I was bitter and angry with her. I could try to act different for periods of time, but eventually something would happen that released my pent up anger. Often it was alcohol. But now there seemed to be a glimmer of light, and it wasn't in her direction. It came from the Kashinska house. It was an escape hatch from all that happened in my house. Even though the motorcycle offered an escape to freedom from the house, the prospect of finally moving from the lake house seemed to feel really good. I saw hope for a new beginning.

The avalanche was set in motion. The eventual proceeds from the sale of the lake house offered enough to allow me to pay off Sylvia and still keep the Kashinska house as well as its adjoining property. Based on my calculations, however, I would need a mortgage that would stretch my financial limits. I would be strapped. I didn't want to be strapped. But the beauty of the Kashinska house held me captive. Perhaps I could sell one of the lots. The eighteen acres naturally divided into three lots with the dividing lines falling between the ravines. If I kept the front two lots, and sold off the back lot, I could live in the house and afford a reasonable mortgage. The house and its adjoining buildings were on the front lot. Eventually, I even planned to sell the front house and build a new house for the kids and myself in the middle lot. I went as far as physically drawing a set of architectural plans. I felt attached to the middle lot, as it was the one I was supposed to purchase if Chris's offer had followed through. But now I was the developer. It had always been a dream of mine to be a land developer and builder. It looked like that dream might now actually come true. It was the first time I was able to dream of a future in years. Life was feeling good.

Further on the downhill slope of the avalanche was fitting better into my shoes, in a figurative sense. The house seemed to fit me better. One of the problems with the lake house was I felt it screamed, "I have money," in an audacious sort of way. Its tall posture, with its roof deck, offered a commanding view of the beaches of Lake Michigan, which could be seen from nearly one mile away. I never felt comfortable with that image. The Kashinska house was merely an old Wisconsin farmhouse nestled among surrounding woodlands. Although the house itself was sizable, it managed to provide the space I needed for raising three children in a less assuming way.

I also saw potential in its layout. During my second walkthrough, I focused on what I could do to make the plan more manageable for my lifestyle. My children were getting older, and soon they would have a need to carve out their own space. I realized the large 1950s addition, with its massive stone fireplace, was set far apart from the rest of the living spaces.

What if I partitioned off the space to create my own private owner's suite? One of the problems of the lake house was it didn't offer enough privacy. As the spaces flowed from one room to another, everyone was aware of everyone's presence all the time. The Kashinska house offered the opportunity to separate kids space from adult space. It seemed like a good opportunity.

The last aspect of the good fit was its age. My new biological roots, which extended deep into American history, felt like a good fit to the house's pre–Civil War origins. Prior to my discovery, my familial roots stretched back to the start of the twentieth century. Both of my parents' families were relatively new comers to this country. Each could find their boat ride within two to three generations. Somehow my newly discovered 1640 roots heard a calling for the solid historic feel to this 1860 stone farmstead. In many ways, the move seemed to follow a natural path.

As we worked out the details of the purchase agreement, Lee Kashinska, the previous owner's son and executive to the estate, wanted to rent the property until the end of summer to complete his final cleanup. This was fine with me as I already had a place to live, and the thought of a summer move was much more palatable than a winter move. It also gave me time to start packing. When Sylvia left, we hadn't even completed the cleanup from the last move. I needed months of sorting and tossing in order to be prepared for my next move. It would also allow the sorting of her stuff versus mine to occur with less friction and hopefully less animosity. I had long ago learned in addition to the kids, possession division was a battleground for divorcing couples. Lee also agreed that I could do some of the remodeling in the house before our arrival.

Much of the late winter and early spring was spent on moving preparation with little attention paid toward finding Ron. Periodically, I would complete another internet search followed by a round of futile calls. I continued discussions with Pat both via the internet and phone. As she had been through several divorces, she was both insightful and comforting. But it was apparent she hadn't budged on her desire to maintain her break with Ron and the rest of the Owens family. Her only contact was with distant relatives on the Owens family website. Once we had firmly identified my place in the Owens family tree, distant second cousins and other relatives fell into place. It was refreshing to move my focus from the cesspool of anger in the various adoption websites, which focused on legal constraints, to the intrigue of the genealogists, who seemed more interested in a new twist to their family tree. To them, I wasn't a bastard child—just another branch that had been discovered. I also made another startling discovery.

TISH THE DISH

As late winter began to fade into spring, my desire to take a break from the endless task of sorting, boxing and tossing all our possessions began to sprout. I had exhausted the local places in Belgium and the surrounding areas and was unable to reliably count on my bike, as the roads were a disastrous mixture of salt, slush and ice. I decided to venture into Port Washington, the next larger town to the south. My destination was Schooner Pub. Port Washington was a historic Wisconsin town located in a quiet harbor on Lake Michigan. It actually contains the largest collection of intact pre–Civil War buildings in the United States. Schooner Pub celebrates Port Washington's rich heritage as a fishing town. Today Port's reality is a busy Lake Michigan tourist destination via boat. In the winter, however, it reverts to a sleepy little burg with a series of pubs known to draw an interesting cross section of society. Besides, Schooner offered a great selection of microbrews.

I had become familiar with Schooner several years ago, when a cousin, Tim, was resolving his brother, Shawn's, estate. Following a John Cougar concert in Milwaukee, Shawn, an avid boater, headed back to his hometown of Port Washington by himself. Against his girlfriend's better judgment, he didn't recognize the hazards of boating alone at night on Lake Michigan. The following day his boat was found revolving in tight circles approximately seven miles off shore, between Milwaukee and Port

Washington. Shawn's body was never found. Tim moved from the East Coast to Wisconsin to clean up Shawn's house and resolve the estate. Periodically, Tim and I would meet at Schooner Pub to wash away the day's work. At that time I thought Tim was a "regular" cousin. Tim was one of the few cousins who didn't know of my birth status. The owner of the bar was named Chico and frequently tended bar. The only thing I liked better than Chico's choices of specialty microbrews was his taste in bartenders. Chico had good taste.

It was a Friday evening around nine, and the crowd had begun to pick up steam. As I was in my midforties, I definitely fell on the older side of the patrons. But directly to the south of the downtown district, a power plant was being reconstructed, and the local ironworkers flooded into Port Washington after work. Many approached my age, but few could beat me in a game of 1960s *Trivial Pursuit*, as for me it was a life experience, not a textbook memory. I glanced to the bar and saw a stool opening up, which I quickly claimed.

"Hey, what can I get ya?" inquired a familiar voice.

"What do you have on tap?"

"Well, give it a shot, and I'll see if I can get it."

"How about an Anchor Steam?"

"You got it."

The problem was the face wasn't familiar. I wished it were. But the truth was, I had never seen her before. Long legs tapered into a slim waist, melded with long, flowing brown hair with blond highlights. To top all that, crystal clear baby blues sat deeply inset into a perfectly chiseled face. I was instantly in lust. Chico came through. At least I thought the few character lines on her face suggested she had been out of high school longer than I'd been teaching it. Even though I knew this had nothing to do with reality, I thought it was worth an evening of self-indulged fantasy. Besides, in two days I'd be Mr. Mom again. After what seemed to be an all too short evening involving way too many Anchor Steams and innocent, irrelevant conversations, I mustered up the courage to ask her name.

"Tish," she responded. I had met Tish the Dish.

The next several months were spent with many nights packing, followed by treks down to Schooner. Bill was always more than eager to meet me at Schooner. I would occasionally happen upon Tish. Bill liked Tish, just like everyone else. When Tish wasn't tending bar, I would get to know Chico's other Port Washington finds. Chico really did have good taste. Chico must have had many divorced male friends, as he seemed to understand his market well. When I could, I would ride the bike down. Regardless of whether I had the bike, my regular outfit typically had some Harley insignia on it. After all, I was a biker, and Damn It the world better know it. Eventually, I came to know Tish was a Harley girl. She loved riding on bikes, but Harley was her only flavor. I also came to know that Tish was the female equivalent of Ollie. She knew everyone. And everyone was in lust with Tish. She was a dish. Tish was going out with Eric.

Sylvia and I continued to visit Dr. Trott. Sometimes it actually seemed like we were making progress, but often it was followed by further clarification of how far apart we actually drifted. The kids seemed to be acclimating to the split family routine. While it wasn't the family I dreamed of in my youth, I began to realize I was not immune to the perils that nearly 50 percent of American families had drifted into. Given my late discovery, I decided it was the least of consequences I could have expected. Each of the kids visited Dr. Trott per his suggestion, and he seemed to concur that all the kids were adapting fairly well. I was on my road to Divorce. It really wasn't as bad as I envisioned. Every now and then, Sylvia and I would seem to have a moment of connection, but it didn't seem to equal the feelings I experienced with my friends on the road. I was moving on. It was time to move on.

In May 2004, I realized I had been able to ride the motorcycle during every month throughout the winter. I also realized I needed to do something about my limbo marriage. I referred to myself as being stuck in limbo land. I had to admit I preferred limbo land to abandon land. I recognized Sylvia and I had entered the same marriage she had witnessed throughout her adolescence and early adulthood. We were indefinitely separated. I could easily have followed the path of least resistance. Her parents were separated for over eight years before they eventually divorced. Their lives were independent, but legally they were still bound by the laws of marriage. In the meantime, her father bore another child from a woman outside their marriage. I decided that would not by my path. Given my options, my only option was opting out. I decided I was the one who needed to file for divorce.

Actually, finding my biological roots contained many divorces helped. Now I wasn't from a family of intact marriages, but one of many failed marriages. My biological father had two marriages not including his bastard child, maybe even more children for all I knew at this point. His mother had five marriages. My biological aunt Pat had three, and from what she told me, Ron was currently on his third. One of my biological father's aunts, Great-Aunt Millie, went as far as fifteen. Even my wife was ending her second. Why was I so afraid of divorce? It was time. *Get over it, Fred. Or was it Steve?* I wasn't sure. All I did know was it was time to file for divorce.

PUTTING AN END TO IT

In May 2004, I filed for divorce from my wife. It was the newest worst day of my life. How could I do this to my children? I was condemning them to a life they didn't ask for. I had to. I made a vow to love her forever—for worse or for better. That was a matter of public record. This was definitely worse. It was my only option. I didn't ask for this hand in the card game, but fuck that! I hadn't asked for a lot of the hands I'd been dealt. I knew I still had a good life, but why the fuck was all this shit happening? I was angry. Fuck that bitch! How could she do this to the kids? How could she do this to me? I wanted life apart from her. I loved her, and she turned on me. I hated her. I filed for divorce.

The Ozaukee County Courthouse was located in Port Washington. It was a beautiful early spring day, so of course I took the bike. I had finished a full day of teaching on a Friday, but I had made the plan. I told

Sylvia earlier in the week of my intentions. Her predictable response was to follow what I thought I needed to do. So I did. It was easier than I imagined. It only took one simple form, and the dastardly deed was done, of course along with a fee. It was way too simple. My first impulse was to head west to the Little Kohler House. A biker bar, nestled in a small burg among the Kettle Moraine, the owner had commiserated with me over many a brew, as he was also in the battles of a divorce. But the scent of Tish drew me eastward to Schooner. How did I know? I haven't a clue. Once I entered Schooner, I saw Hamilton. One of the Union Riders, Hamilton was an Ironworker at the power plant. He stopped by to remedy the toll the day had taken on him. Tish was tending. I originally met Hamilton at the Road House. Together we concocted a scheme to create collapsible bar stools to make cleaning easier, after way to many cocktails. We had bonded.

Tish was in her full glory, but she had few patrons at four in the afternoon to appreciate her. I had battled the better part of five months to gain her attention. Now she was bored. I was there. I had a Harley. It was time for her break. She wanted a ride. Despite the fact I was glad to see a familiar face in Hamilton, she needed a distraction. As I asked Tish for a brew for Hamilton and myself, Tish replied, "You want to go for a quickie?" I wasn't sure what exactly she meant, but I was more than willing to accommodate her needs. I quickly gave Hamilton his beer and proceeded with Tish out to my bike. We cruised around Port and eventually, under her direction, ended up back at Schooner, at which time she gave me a quick peck on the cheek and said, "You're sweet." I was in heaven. Not a bad day for filing divorce. It seemed to be another omen, which I wanted to follow. Tish went from fantasy to possibility.

As early spring progressed into summer, I continued my periodic rides to Port Washington. I also got ready for the end of the school year. Ohio Technical College (OTC) provided a summer education program for tech ed. teachers. One of OTC's programs was specifically tailored to auto body, which I saw as an opportunity to figure out a cheap way to fix the self-inflicted dents in my motorcycle gas tank. I talked to Sylvia about working out the details of childcare duties and decided to make it a go. As it was in Cleveland, I also saw it as an opportunity to try to connect with John and Guy. But John had moved back to Arizona. This time it seemed like Guy was more receptive, so I jumped on the opportunity. I made plans to take the Lake Michigan Ferry from Milwaukee to Muskegon and ride the bike over to the program, with a stop overnight in Toledo. It would be the first long road trip I had planned to take on the bike, and I would be taking it alone. While part of me was nervous about traveling so far alone on the bike, I felt we had become quite acclimated, as I managed to put on just under fifteen thousand miles in my first year in the saddle. I thought I was ready for a road trip.

Sylvia and I had been talking more and actually doing less marriage counseling. Dr. Trott had moved to a position of encouraging me to move on. To me, it seemed he was getting ready to close the file. I was also getting ready to move. Lee indicated he would be leaving in early summer, and I was ready to start the remodeling. I had shown Sylvia the house and the land, and she seemed intrigued by the project. Sylvia had agreed to move into the lake house after I left to save on rent expense. The separation had started to take its toll on our finances. We had decided to try moving ahead with the divorce without a lawyer. We both were far more distrustful of lawyers than either of us were of each other. Wisconsin required a six-month cooling-down period from the date of filing. We were also required to take a parenting as a single parent class. Based on my calculations, we would be divorced by early August.

GUY AND THE AVENGERS

The school year ended, and I packed my bike for the trip. As I didn't want to miss my ferry ride, I made sure I arrived at the ferry terminal a couple of hours early. Once I checked in, I decided to head to a local coffee shop for a bite to eat before my journey. The terminal was located in an up-and-coming area just south of downtown Milwaukee, which was experiencing revitalization. As I received my order, I couldn't help but notice a commotion just outside the coffee shop. A van, which proudly declared its contents in bold letters read "Feingold." Sure enough, Senator Russ Feingold emerged and proceeded into the coffee shop. After an introduction Senator Feingold remarked that he sure would appreciate me spreading a good word among the bikers. He felt the majority of bikers tended to lean to the Right. I think he was correct. Once he left I called Sylvia to tell her of my encounter. As a Far Left Democrat, I thought she would appreciate the experience. I was right. She found it fascinating and was interested in the details of what he said. In some ways, I think she was surprised and rather pleased I took the time to call her and tell her about my encounter. It may have been a baby step forward.

Soon the ship was loaded and on its way to Michigan. From the observation deck on top of the boat, I watched the Milwaukee skyline disappear. I also felt the burden of everything back there sink below the horizon. I was free. I wasn't a bastard. I wasn't a father. I wasn't a husband in a failing marriage. I was me. It felt good. During the two-hour ride across the lake, for the better part of an hour there was no land in sight. There seemed to be no future nor any past. The present was all there was. Once I deboarded the boat in Michigan, I began my journey into the future. It was the journey to get to know my half brother Guy. At that point I realized this would be as close as I would be able to come to have any insight into what Don was like. Regina described him as a little Don. I wondered what she meant by that. I guess I would find out.

Riding bike around the eastern shores of Lake Michigan was an experience to behold. Enormous sand dunes partitioned the expansive bays, punctuated with older resort towns. While the western shores of the lake in Wisconsin were certainly beautiful, the dramatic combination of dunes, water, and forest made the ride on the bike seem like an altered experience. The weather was on my side, as the forecast called for a midseventies, partly cloudy day. It was perfect road-tripping weather. As the sun eventually traveled from being my destination to my departure, I was nearing the Ohio border. It was time to call Guy. He was working that afternoon but had arranged to be off work and was free of childcare that evening. A plan was made. I would call him after I settled in, and we would grab a bite to eat at a bar and grill nearby. As he was aware I was coming in on a bike, he planned to take me to a local biker party. Although he didn't have a bike, he found the crowd fascinating. Maybe it was a commonality.

Our dinner together was interesting but fairly uneventful, with the exception of Guy's romantic interests. It seemed Guy was quite the ladies' man. Several attractive young women joined us at the bar. Watching him in action provided insight into how he had managed to acquire his followers as well as several offspring outside the confines of marriage. It seemed my younger brother was teaching me lessons in alternate family structures. Maybe this is what Regina meant. Guy showed no hesitation in describing our relationship to each other, and he almost seemed to take pride in it. He, too, seemed to be fascinated by common features and mannerisms we shared. As we concluded our dinner and proceeded to the biker party, we had a chance to talk about Don. Guy was two when Regina moved away. He had no memory of Don and chose to not think about him. On the other hand, his relationship with Don, or lack thereof, seemed to be a driving force in how he would deal with the fact he had children from extramarital affairs. He would be financially responsible and would continue to be an active force in his kids' lives.

Given Guy's lack of biking experience, he was fairly unaware of exactly what kind of party we were going to. It was a club party. I had experience with club parties and was a bit hesitant about attending one without much knowledge about the club. Club parties varied in their composition, but all of them shared the common ingredients of a lot of men in black, a virtual ocean of alcohol, and often an extensive collection of female mammary glands. Despite their reputations, I rarely experienced the fights and brawls, which are an assumed ingredient. Periodically, the combination of the first two ingredients would lead to disputes over the last ingredient, but typically the organizing club would step in with their "security" force to resolve the matter. Their security force was always comprised of very large males given a wide range of discretion on how exactly the matters would be resolved. As Guy had clearly displayed his appetite for the last ingredient of biker parties, and we were already well on our way to consuming too much of the second, I didn't want to become a problem.

The Avengers were an Ohio-based club, with franchises in several of the neighboring states. I wasn't familiar with the Avengers, as they hadn't made it into Wisconsin yet. Their compound was extensive. It came complete with a campground, clubhouse that resembled a Boy Scout mess hall with a bar, a large, sheltered amphitheater, and a playground. What was a playground doing in a biker compound? As we mingled among the participants, we came to learn the Avengers were a family-friendly biking club. It was a new type of club to me. The vast majority of clubs I had experienced were far from family friendly. While the party came complete with a halftime show centered on the third ingredient, it seemed most of the year the compound was used by its extensive membership base as a place to take the family camping. I became intrigued by the concept of weaving my newly formed identity as a biker with my family. Guy had shown me a good time.

The following morning, I continued my road trip to Cleveland. Another beautiful day led the way for my ride along the southern shores of Lake Erie. The trip had already been a great success, even though it was only the beginning. While I had only traveled a little over three hundred miles on the bike, I had covered thousands in my head. Hours alone on the bike allowed me to rehash and reweave many loose ends, which were waiting to unravel. In addition, the new ingredients of a relationship with Guy and the family-friendly biking club allowed me to reframe many of the old images of my past and paint new visions of my future. Once again the future was looking bright.

The rest of the trip was uneventful. Among the participants were many divorced males. It seemed the tech ed. field experienced a fairly high incidence of divorce. I even happened upon another adoptee who was in the process of a search. While he was aware of his adoption from his earliest recollection, like so many adoptees, it wasn't until later in life as he saw his own children grow that he turned toward the path of discovering his own biological past. He, too, ran into the endless antiquated laws of discrimination, prohibiting his search. While he was frustrated, his batteries still held enough juice to continue his mission.

I returned home on a Sunday and quickly assumed my parenting responsibilities. My time away had left Sylvia with the kids without any breaks for the week. Even though we had been on an every other week schedule, we each took a kid or two on the other's shift for some alone time. It was Sylvia's idea, and it turned out to be a good one. Prior to our separation, time spent with the kids was an all-or-nothing proposition, allowing the other to have a bit of a respite. Now each of the kids could spend some alone time with one parent at a time. Sylvia was also planning a trip to Pennsylvania over the week of the Fourth of July with the kids to see her family. As a result, our schedule of kid duty had fallen into a bit more of a random pattern. We were starting to work together on something, even if it was a divorce. Unfortunately, her trip would coincide with my upcoming move and her moving back into the lake house. We still didn't have any viable buyers for the lake house, and it seemed since we had two houses it made the most financial sense for us each to live in one.

Over the course of the summer, I eventually came to realize Tish was not interested in me, at least for now, but she did bring me into her fold. I had become one of her studs. "Sunday is fun day," was Tish's motto, as she never worked on Sundays. While I didn't realize it from the patron standpoint, I soon realized it from the friend of Tish's viewpoint. Although I didn't make it as Tish's designated boy toy, I did make it as her second tier. I learned Tish's hierarchy. I was now second string. She had broken up with Eric and was now on the prowl for a new boy toy. Chad eventually became her new boy toy. As second string, I was constantly set up with new riders. One week it was Christie, the next Amy. I actually liked being a potential boy toy. Amy gave great back massages, and it had nothing to do with her hands.

Bill and I had enjoyed many alcohol-saturated rides together. One Sunday afternoon we decided to meet in Adell. Adell was located on a crossroad between my house, his house, and the Road House. When I arrived, Amy was there with a friend. Amy had a body Marilyn Monroe would envy, but unfortunately her friend could push my shocks to the limit. When Bill arrived, we all decided to ride to the Road House for the open jam, their regular Sunday event. Honda's have always been known for their durability, and luckily Amy's friend decided on "blurple," the color of Bill's ride. Besides, any friend of Tish's would never be caught dead on anything less than a Harley.

SETTLING INTO NEW DIGS

Moving weekend came and went. I used Hamilton, Bill, and Hap for my brawn. All were sizable, and despite the enormity of the job it went fairly smoothly. I also managed to help Sylvia get from her apartment into the lake house. Once in my new home, I started to clear trails on the land. In many ways, it was similar to the thickets I had cut my way through at the cabin. This time, however, I was cutting through the thickets of my embattled relationship with Sylvia. I had a final session with Dr. Trott, and he questioned why I held on so long. Many others would have given up long ago. My answer was, "I guess, when it came down to it, I loved her." I still hadn't let go. I wanted to, but I couldn't. I decided I still had to try. In the middle of a thicket, my phone rang. Sylvia wanted to come over and discuss something. Did she want to return home? Maybe there was hope after all. I told her where I was on the land. It could be such a happy ending. When she found me in the thicket, she had an energetic look. She was happy. She wanted to buy a home in Cedar Grove for herself. I was devastated.

Another Fourth of July weekend was here, and Sylvia was off to Pennsylvania for the holiday. Even though we had been getting along better, I still wasn't invited. But she managed to leave the final cleanup of her apartment for me. It seemed like my role in her life was cleaning up her messes. I accepted it, after all, she did bear me three beautiful children. I'd be there when she needed me, but I didn't see any hope for us anymore.

I was through.

When I didn't have the kids, most of my nights were spent getting ready for their next visit, followed by trips to the Lake Church Inn or Port Washington. It was a big old farmhouse, and when I was there alone I was lonely. A singer named Dido had recently released a song titled "White Flag." It was about someone who refused to surrender in a hopeless relationship. I related to the song. After nights of socializing, I would often crash on the couch in the living room instead of making my way up to the second-floor bedroom I had made mine. Occasionally, I would wake up in the middle of the night, at random times, and mysteriously Dido would be bellowing "White Flag" to me on the boom box in the kitchen. Was it a fluke of the boom box? I haven't a clue. To this day, I still suspect it was the spirit of Clare or Eleanor Kashinska, the previous owners, urging me to hold on to hope.

The second half of Sylvia's trip was far more interesting for me. Many of my biking friends from ABATE were attending Iowa's ABATE state meeting, a weekend party in Algona, Iowa. Once my duties were done, I packed my bike and once again headed off to meet them. I was late to arrive at our rendezvous, and I found out that was a crime. I was in the doghouse. I should have recognized it as foreshadowing of things to come. When we reached Algona, we quickly found our designated area and set up camp. There was partying to be done! This was not an Avenger's party, as there were no families in sight. Rain the day before left too many opportunities for rolls in the mud, which were done. Before I knew it a close friend's wife had gone too far after too much of the second ingredient of a biker party, and I was about to become the center of a confrontation.

Biker clubs really aren't that different from other organizations in that they need new blood to ensure the existence of a future. I was a big, well built, bald headed, tattooed Harley rider who looked like someone who would be an asset in a group brawl. And I could hold my liquor with the best of them. I was a desirable recruit. One of the leaders from a group interested in having me join their ranks suggested to his wife that she show me some hospitality. Whereas I thought I might have a viewing as to what was under those leathers, I had no idea how she interpreted hospitality. Before I knew it her tongue took a tour of my face using figure-eight patterns ending in my ear while her fingers explored a meandering path headed for the southern border. It instantly became clear the leader's interpretation of hospitality was more in alignment with mine, and he immediately made his disapproval known both verbally and physically. Groups and alliances became apparent as colors banded together in defensive postures. I instantly learned what starts biker brawls.

This wasn't what I was looking for, and soon my flight response kicked into high gear. I was on the road once again. Unfortunately, it was midnight, and all the rooms were filled for at least a hundred-mile radius as a result of the gathering. It was a long night on the bike. Eventually, I found a room on the Wisconsin border. Once again Dorothy was glad to be heading toward Kansas. Morning was a relief. I was a bit hungover, but my anticipation of getting to the safe haven of home energized me. As I rode, I recollected the time I spent with Guy. My Algona experience was so different from my Avengers experience. I liked the Avengers. It was more me. I wasn't Algona. It was awful. I missed the kids. I even missed Sylvia.

CHAPTER 8

THE WINDS OF CHANGE
AUGUST 2004

Something must have happened on Sylvia's trip as well. She had changed. When she returned home, she was more engaging and didn't bring up her desire to buy her own home anymore. As a matter of fact, she was helping with my house. Getting the kids settled in and unpacking was an overwhelming task. Everything needed to be done immediately. As we worked on the house together, we began to talk—at first a little, but then it was a lot. Within a few weeks, we were on the road to reconciliation. She decided she would be willing to give our relationship a try again in the new house. We needed to plan another move. While I had come to find positive aspects to my new life outside an intact family, I recognized I really did still love Sylvia. The winds of change now blew in a favorable direction. I filed a motion to end the divorce proceedings. It was two weeks before our final hearing date. We came very close.

We decided to move back together before the new school year started to make the transition easier for the kids. As Sylvia hadn't been in the lake house with the kids very long, much of their stuff was still packed. But we did keep most of our furniture in the lake house to show better. As we talked, we decided we needed to sell the house fast to stop the exorbitant interest costs of the bridge loan. My uncle Joe had used a Realtor named Dina Bassette several times and claimed she could sell anything quickly and get a great price. We decided to give her a try. Dina came in with a few "small detail" suggestions, which were quickly implemented. We awaited Dina's magic.

Unfortunately, another change was about to take place. For years Sylvia had been complaining about stomach issues, and she decided to finally investigate. It turned out Sylvia needed a medical procedure. She scheduled a date around teacher's convention to minimize her days off. Her surgery date came and went, and soon she was healing and gradually getting her strength back. We all were on the road to recovery. The kids had gotten back to their old bickering patterns, but in the new house there were places to seek refuge. Sylvia was able to recover in the master suite, while World War III occurred on the second floor. It seemed the configuration of the new house would better accommodate our lifestyle. It felt good to be a family.

As Sylvia started feeling better, she gradually took on more projects in the new house. Virtually every surface needed to be reworked. I was focusing on the finishing work as the result of the remodeling and the floors, Sylvia was getting the kitchen sorted and painting the halls. Initially, I moved the three kids into one bedroom together, as I completed work on the other two. After all, while living in Sylvia's apartment, they all shared a single room with much less common space. Gradually, the diamond made it from the coal seam into the rough. Sylvia seemed to be flourishing in her new environment.

Joe was right; Dina came through. The buyers were from Chicago, offered a good price, made a cash offer, and wanted immediate possession.

We were elated. The financial burden of the bridge loan had started to become a stress point. We were using a home equity line of credit to finance the payments on both the new mortgage as well as the bridge loan on the lake house. After a few months, it became evident that the bridge loan was a path to financial ruin. We also came to the conclusion the cabin would have to go. Since I discovered my bike, I had made few trips up north, and the trips were only to perform the necessary maintenance. I also realized the work required in the new house would keep me occupied for the better part of next five years. Additionally, the new place had eighteen acres of wilderness woodlands. My experience having the cabin provided insight. Everyone headed up north to hunt. We lived in a protected area where the deer thrived as a result of the adjoining cornfields. We lived in a hunter's paradise. Since there were more deer in my backyard than in 160 acres up north, we didn't need a hunting cabin, as we lived in one. We contacted the agent in Pembine, Wisconsin, through whom we originally purchased the property, and it went on the market. We were just heading into hunting season, so it seemed like it would be a good time to sell.

It had been nearly two years since I located Pat and made any progress on locating Don. I began to accept the fact I would never find out what happened to him, or if I had any other siblings. While it wasn't a good feeling, there was an aspect to it that brought some resolution. I realized I couldn't let it take me down. I needed to focus on my immediate family and not get side tracked from Sylvia, the kids, and building a new life together. Sylvia was seeming to pick up steam. Something in the new house brought her to a place of happiness. In many regards, it was similar to the first house we purchased together in Minnesota—a 1927 white-stucco bungalow on Ivy Lane. The new home was bigger, but some of the charm of a bygone era was exhibited in both this house and the Ivy Lane House. Not only did the house fit me better but it also seemed to capture the best of Sylvia. Once again I wondered if it was Clare and Eleanor.

As fall eased into winter and I continued to cut my way through the thickets and gathered wood for fires, I discovered another wonderful aspect to the house. The massive stone fireplace was capable of holding two full sized fireplace grates and had incorporated the fireplace into the master's suite. As the fires burned away a day's work of gathering wood into a spectacular blaze, Sylvia and I rekindled our feelings for each other. I loved Sylvia, and she loved me. Once again we were all happy.

PART III

NEW INSIGHTS
FROM THE PAST

CHAPTER 9

RECONNECTING

May 2005

Life moved on. The holidays came and went, we chiseled away on the projects in the house, and the kids readapted to life in a nuclear family. We even managed to sell the cabin. While I had made a conscious effort to continue to see my friends on the road, it seemed the divorced crowd really didn't relate to reconciled couples. Besides, given the magnitude of projects in the new house, I really didn't have the time to get out on the bike as much either. I promised myself I would resurrect my interest in the spring.

During the Mother's Day Saturday every year, Belgium held its town rummage sale. It's a big event for the town, and the spring of 2005 must have had at least one hundred participating households. Typically, I didn't attend the event, as I do not like crowds, and I detest shopping. But that morning Tony wanted a breakfast kringle from the gas station, and Sylvia had already started her painting project for the day. I decided my best strategy was to accommodate Tony's desires. As I approached Belgium, I saw the multitudes already lining the streets at nine. In the back of my mind, I recollected to the time Sylvia bought into the concept of snowmobiles. She only bought into the idea once the option of her having her own came into play. Perhaps motorcycles held the same key. Maybe if she could have her own motorcycle, Sylvia would be more open to the sport. Riding certainly opened a whole new life for me, so maybe it would do the same for her. I decided to do a quick cruise through the streets of Belgium to see if there were any motorcycles on the sales block. After a few turns down crowded streets, I spotted Sylvia's motorcycle. It was a Honda V-max 500. The beauty was it was a Honda. Sylvia owned a Honda Accord before we married, which she coveted to that day. Sylvia held a lot of faith in the Honda Motor Company, and maybe she would be open to this bike. I retrieved my kringle from the gas station, delivered it to Tony, and told Sylvia of my find. I was right. She was willing to take a look.

When we approached the bike, the owner quickly appeared. Actually, it wasn't the owner, but his father's. Being a 1988, it was a bit older, but it was in immaculate condition, and it had lower miles. Further discussion revealed it was JJ's bike. JJ was a graduate of Cedar Grove–Belgium High School, who I had for several classes, and his father was on the school board. Unfortunately, my wife was the one who was politically astute in the family, and I wasn't even aware that Jeff, JJ's father, was a school board member. After a test drive, we made an offer and acquired the bike. Before we left, Jeff indicated JJ would be back later that day, and we could sign the title. I agreed to come over when he called. Sylvia was excited to try her new bike, and I was excited she was excited.

Later that day, JJ called, and he was ready. When I arrived, I was surprised at JJ. Students mature so much in the immediate years following high school, and JJ was not an exception. He was a young man and wanted to sell the bike, as he had just acquired a beefier Honda 1000 crotch rocket. Both his father and mother were worried, as it was a very powerful bike, and they were afraid it would bring him harm. JJ desperately wanted me to give his new bike a try, and I accommodated his wishes. It was a monster. A simple touch of the throttle sent the back wheels screaming. It was a very powerful bike. After I returned the bike back to JJ, I warned him to be careful. I also thanked him for his bike, and indicated it was for my wife, Sylvia. He seemed pleased it found a good home. It had been a good bike to him. It was the last time I saw JJ alive.

I taught Sylvia the basics in the yard. Our yard contained the better part of three acres of mowed motorcycle-learning ground. As I couldn't bear the thought of watching her dump the bike, each time I started her off on a new lesson I purposefully went out of sight to do other tasks. At first her task was shifting from first into second. Eventually, she was making elongated figure eights in the yard, with many shifts in between. She took the motorcycle class and passed. She was becoming a biker. I was happy.

It wasn't that I needed her to be a biker more that I wanted to see her happy. I felt a lot of our separation had to do with her being unhappy, and I didn't want to see that happen again. I was happy to be together again as an intact family and wanted it to stay that way. My bike brought me much happiness, but I wasn't sure if it would do the same for her. I had long been a fan of motor sports, but she always seemed hesitant. I also thought this would be the perfect way to meld our two different worlds into one. The kids were getting older, so it seemed this could be something that we could do together without the kids. From the day we started having children, our alone time was what we gave up. That was one of her biggest complaints in counseling, so I thought this could be something to accommodate her needs. It would be something we could do together without the kids.

OUT OF NOWHERE
(MAY 2005)

At long last it was time for the anticipated Memorial Day weekend. Every teacher knew it was a time to behold. The insanity will soon stop, and all will have a break from the chaos of a school year that had simply gone on too long. The school year has cycles, and the final cycle of the year ends with the Memorial Day weekend. Unfortunately, in the high school, the time from spring break until the Memorial Day weekend was the period of the final senior burnout. The seniors had long ago moved past the anticipation of their future life and started to live them. It was time to pull out the whips and start the beatings. Of course, that's meant figuratively, not literally. But the simple truth was, the seniors had shut down, and they set the tone for the rest of the school. I was ready for summer. The year had taken its life's course, and the corpse was ready to be buried. When I returned from the holiday weekend, I completed my usual ritual of firing up my computer and checking my email. There lay two treasures. The first was an email from Pat. The second was one from Ron Bracken. The subject line read: "Don's Brother."

I was in shock. Was this the Ron Bracken I had been seeking for the better part of the last four years? Who else could it be? I skipped Pat's email and went directly to Ron's. As I read it, I suddenly became afraid I would die before I had a chance to finish it. Ron contacted Pat over the Memorial Day weekend, and she had told him about me. He wanted me to contact him. He was anxious to talk to me. The bell rang, and it was time to start my first hour. I was brought back to the earlier days of give them something to do so I could get on with life. Fortunately, I had planned for my first hour to complete chapter questions. I was relieved. As the students completed their work, I frantically typed out an email. Somewhere in between a plea for mercy and a cry for help, I'm sure Ron got the impression I was more than anxious to talk to him. He responded within a few minutes. I was live with Uncle Ron, the brother of Don Brookshier. He was the only one who held the answers. He was the only one who could finally close the book. I had no idea where this would lead. I would soon find out.

MORE THAN ANSWERS

Once again the adoption gods were with me. I called Ron when I got home after school. Ron was an open book. God, I loved the Owenses. They may have had many failed marriages, but they sure didn't hold any stigmas about bastards. Not only was he forgiving about my intrusions but also he was actually excited. He loved his brother and felt my existence was a blessing. The final years of Don's life had always been a bit of a mystery to him. He felt there was a sadness about Don, but wasn't sure exactly what it was. In retrospect, he thought it began around the time I was born. He admitted Don never told him about my existence. It didn't matter. He was glad I was alive.

Don stayed in the Chicago area after Regina left him. Ron indicated they had a tumultuous marriage, and Don even questioned the paternity of his children. Obviously, Don also had trust issues. It seems to have run in the family. Don eventually started driving cab in the Des Plains area. He died picking up a fare in the lobby of a hotel on his route. He died at the age of sixty of a sudden heart attack and many attended his funeral. He never married again nor had additional children, at least as far as Ron knew. But I realized Ron didn't know about me either, so he could be off on that one. Ron recalled one weekend he, Don, and Don's kids went to the Milwaukee County Zoo. He remembered the kids were fairly young, but he thought John had to be at least nine or ten. While his story didn't coincide with Regina's account of her total cutoff from Don, I never pursued the issue. I wondered if Don and my half brothers were actually at the Milwaukee County Zoo at the same time as I was. After all, I grew up close to the zoo and spent many days there. Ron also indicated that Don spent a lot of time at the Arlington Horse Racing Track betting on the ponies. It was another potential encounter. My parents frequented the Arlington track, and periodically brought me with them. I had a vague recollection of seeing a man I was intrigued with at the track when I was young. Was it Don? Ron answered a lot of questions, but at the same time opened the door to so many more.

Ron and I continued a flurry of emails and conversations over the next several weeks. As I got to know Ron, I recognized something very familiar within him. Many aspects of his personality seemed to reflect mine. An interesting comment Ron made was that Don's phone voice sounded just like John Wayne. He further indicated from the moment he spoke to me on the phone he knew I was his son, as I sounded like Don but without his Missouri accent. At last I seemed to find the familiar comfort I had so desperately been seeking for the last forty-five years. He felt like family.

While my adoptive family provided love and comfort, I always seemed to experience a void. I loved them. They loved me. But something was missing. Familial bonds grow deep. There is something beyond the surface that seems to touch the heart and soul. Family knows they are family. The saying blood is thicker than water is not accidental; as a matter of fact, it's very insightful. It reflects an inner soul being as familiar with another soul that it is with itself.

As Ron and I continued to move forward with our discussions, Ron told me of Don's boss, Roy Vanna, owner of the Friendly Cab Company of Des Plains, Illinois. Again I wondered. Had I run into Don at the O'Hare Airport in Des Plains when I lived in Rockford and traveled in and out of O'Hare? As we talked further, I could tell that Roy loved Don, and Don loved Roy. Don had become part of Roy's family. Ron also told me of trips he and Don shared, along with Don's eventual desire to move to Colorado, where Ron lived at the time. Ron's discussions were both insightful and heartfelt. I could tell Ron truly loved Don as only a brother could. I could also tell Ron was starting to love me as only an uncle could. It was a good feeling. I began to feel the same toward him. God, it felt good to find Ron.

Unfortunately, Ron, too, was experiencing a failing marriage with his third wife, Dianna. They had only been married a couple of years, and already it had grown stale. She was high-maintenance, and he wanted out. His biggest issue was she was driving a wedge between him and his kids. Initially, they all seemed to get along fairly well, but as time went on she grew indifferent and the kids grew resentful. He no longer loved her and wanted to find a way to end it, but didn't know how. It seemed he was following the Owens's pattern. I was intrigued. Did this pattern seem to follow an invisible path oblivious to adoption? I had meandered down a path that led to those feelings. Mine seemed to find resolve, but was that because a different family raised me? The questions seemed endless. I was mystified.

Ron's oldest son. Sean, and his wife, Heather, lived in New Orleans. Sean had become a prominent lawyer, and they were looking forward to expanding their family. Unfortunately, another event would side track their plans. Hurricane Katrina hit New Orleans and suddenly Ron found himself living with some of the refugees, along with their two rottweilers. Ron enjoyed the diversion. But it seemed to take the final toll on Dianna, and she headed to her hometown in Colorado.

In the meantime, Ron revealed he still had Don's ashes. They were contained in their original mailing box from the crematorium in his office. He indicated that if I wanted them, I was more than welcome to do with them as I saw fit, as he had never decided how to properly dispose of them. Besides, Don's other children, John and Guy, didn't really seem interested in Don's life. I told him I would be more than happy to have Don, as it seemed like it would be an appropriate closure for me. Ron also indicated I could have the rest of Don's possessions he had gathered after Don's funeral. To me, it exceeded my wildest expectations. I was elated.

Ron had three children—my cousins. Sean was the oldest, followed by Joshua, and then Heather. Sean and Joshua were from the same mother. Heather was from Ron's second wife. Like Don and me, Ron had an appetite for beautiful women, and all his children were beautiful. Sean, being a lawyer, was academically successful, as was his last, Heather. Joshua seemed to struggle with high school academics, as did Don as well as myself. I had reading issues when I was younger, as does one of my children, as did Don. It seemed to be a family trait. When Ron married his last wife, he viewed it as his final marriage. After Hurricane Katrina hit, Sean, his wife, and their two dogs moved in. It went from being permanent to temporary.

Ron had given me another loose thread to pull, so I did. Roy Vana lived in Chicago, and I called Roy to arrange a visit. Roy was excited to hear about another chapter about Don's life. He missed Don. Don had been a driver for several years, and "a damn good driver at that." Roy was willing to meet with me, and plans were made. It was early summer and I had a flexible schedule. Although Des Plains had changed quite a bit since Don's death, we met in one of the few remaining establishments since the time of Don's tenure in Des Plains, one of Don's favorite spots, named the Chili Bowl. The Chili Bowl was an interesting combination of a lunch café, with an adjoining bar. We met in the bar.

Don favored beer, and Roy seemed to take great joy in buying me one of Don's favorite taps. It was only eleven when we met, but Roy assured me Don wouldn't have had a problem with having a toast before noon. He proceeded to show me around downtown Des Plains and pointed out many of the places Don liked. Even though Don's apartment building had been razed, he showed me where the building stood. Our final stop was one of the few older taverns where Don was a regular. Roy introduced me to an older gentleman tending bar, explaining I was Don Brookshier's son. At first the bartender seemed confused, but then something seemed to click. It made sense. I looked like him. It was an amazing day.

Through Ron, I was also able to connect with Lee, Don's other half sister. Lee lived in Northern California with Edna, during Edna's final days. I called Lee, and like Ron she was an open book, and an encyclopedia at that. As Lee was older than Ron, Lee's memories of Don growing up were more complete, especially during Don's younger years. Also like Ron, she hadn't a clue I existed. While it seemed on Don's side I was an invisible chapter of Don's life, she like Ron and Pat, welcomed another chapter of their brother's life. They all missed Don. As I got to know Lee through a series of phone conversations, I became aware she typified the California hippy lifestyle. She seemed nomadic in her nature and seemed to be fairly self-sufficient. For a while, like Don, she managed a bar. She also wrote music and even made a record. Lee indicated she never married and had enjoyed living life on her own terms. Ironically, she lived in a town I had once worked in. I had worked for a little hospital just outside Mount Shasta, in Red Bluff, California, as part of a consulting project when I lived in Southern California. Lee lived by Mount Shasta. It was another irony that had been revealed during this long and winding journey as a result of a simple twist of fate.

SUMMER'S LOOSE ENDS

More conversations with Ron continued, and more insights were given, but despite both our efforts no plans were made for me to make it down to Texas to meet him and pick up Don's ashes. In retrospect, I should have made it a higher priority than I did. At the time I think I was basking in the glory of finally finding out what actually happened to Don. When I found out I was adopted, I had managed to find my biological mother in two months. I was lucky. Most adoptees often take years to find their biological mother, if ever at all. Then hopefully if she's cooperative, they'll be told about their biological father. I found my biological mother within two months of starting my search, and then even though he had already died, I found out about my biological father and at least found out about most of his life fairly soon. Compared to those who had dead-ended, and still were searching for their biological mothers, I was very fortunate. I was a very blessed bastard.

Unfortunately, toward the end of the summer, I found out another marriage was heading for an end. John Schmidt stopped by to tell me that he was leaving Martha. As their children left the fold, so, too, did their love for each other. John held it in for years, and when the last of their two children left the nest John decided it was time to make a new life of his own, apart from Martha. After Sylvia and I had finally found a way to keep our lives together, it was hard to see another set of close friends follow a similar destructive path that we had trailed. Martha was destroyed. How could John do this? I related to Martha while Sylvia remained silenced. But wasn't the spouse always the last to know? It seemed I wasn't the only one capable of keeping myself in the dark. It made me realize neither denial nor divorces were isolated to my adoptive situation. It also made me realize that while our marriage may have been headed down a path similar to John and Martha, the crushing weight of a spouse losing the very essence of their foundation, at the very least, expedited our collapse.

The final lessons of the summer of 2005 that shaped a redirection were centered on my road friends. Over the course of the summer, three friends had serious motorcycle accidents. The first was Ollie's wife, Sonya. In the late morning, she was traveling down a rural country road, when an elderly couple suddenly appeared over a hillcrest, backing up in her lane. Her only option was to swerve to the right into an adjacent corn field. While she kept the bike up through most of her detour, the final culvert took its toll, and Sonya flipped off her bike, landing headfirst. She wasn't wearing a helmet. Sonya suffered severe brain damage, in addition to other multiple bodily injuries. Another, Rich was traveling at dusk, when he hit a deer. A few road rashes were the worst of his initial injuries, until the bike behind him ran him over like a speed bump, shattering his leg and entire pelvis. Additionally, Hamilton was critically injured in an accident on his way back from a summer club party. Neither Rich nor Hamilton used helmets, but both, despite critical injuries, were able to eventually make full recoveries. Finally, a couple of weeks after I bought JJ's bike, he was killed on his new bike. During a late-night summer ride, JJ encountered an unexpected fog bank at the bottom of a hill on a backcountry road. JJ met his fate with a tree, which coincidently was located in his uncle's yard. He was the only rider wearing a helmet. I was mortified. His funeral was awful. I didn't tell Sylvia.

As I pondered the deluge of critical injuries and fatal outcomes I witnessed over the course of the summer, I recalled a discussion I had one alcohol saturated evening with Sparky. Many bikers believed helmets were irrelevant. Their lives were on a course directed by fate. Regardless of the severity of the accident, or if they wore a helmet, the outcome was simply the result of fate. Whether it was predetermined or not wasn't the point.

The real issue was more about the purpose, or lack thereof, and was independent of human will or action. It simply occurred.

While getting my motorcycle was initially driven out of a perceived need for balance in my life as my wife was walking out the door, I also started to wonder if it wasn't tied to a greater path fate had led me down. I recalled taking a moon-drenched walk on the beach with Ajax just over a year after Chic's death and shortly before my discovery. At the time I thought I was still mourning Chic's and Nic's death, as my mood was rather sullen. I stopped on the sand, and while watching the pounding waves I asked for truth. I wanted to better understand reality—my reality. Initially, the only change that occurred was the arrival of Luke with his mother within a few days of my nighttime walk. But shortly after that, my entire world turned upside down, and I had a whole new perspective on my truth. Perhaps that was my call for fate to interject and send me on my new path—the path I needed to live. I realized whereas I could dwell on the fact my birth status wasn't at all what I thought it was, and I wasn't who I thought, perhaps it was simply a matter of my newfound friend, fate. I found fatalistic philosophy added a comfort level to the unexpected.

Ron's interjection into my life seemed to fill in the final missing pieces of Don and his family. The picture of my paternal side was fairly full. It was interesting, because I had found so much about my paternal side, but much of my maternal side was still a mystery. I had met my biological mother, not my biological father. But I knew so much more about his side, and very little about hers. Was it because he was dead and she wasn't? Perhaps, but even if he wasn't, would it have mattered? I couldn't be sure. She was what blocked me from knowing her side. Maureen held a shroud of secrecy. It was her shame. She couldn't bear for anyone to know I existed. True, in her closest family, her own children for whom she was the matriarch, I was allowed out of the closet. But for the rest of the family and her closest friends, I still was a deep, dark secret that couldn't be exposed. My identity on her side was held captive by her secret. I detested the thought of having to lie about who I was, but I couldn't face the thought of exposing her. I was the dark stain that must never be exposed to the light of righteousness. Should I be exposed, her life would be condemned to hell, at least the life she created. I was shame. I was her deepest sin. According to the law, it was the life I had to live.

The end of summer also brought the end to Ron's marriage, along with my opportunity to meet Ron and retrieve Don. Throughout the summer, I didn't realize my ability to make it down there was only a window. Ron had to get out in a hurry. All his possessions, along with Don, were packed into a self-storage unit somewhere around Austin, Texas, as he began a period of nomadic travel. Ron was a headhunter, and as long as he had access to the internet, he could continue to do his cyberwork. Once again Ron became elusive, and I had missed my chance and learned a lesson. I decided the next time I had the opportunity to meet Ron and get Don, I would not be as foolish. Other things would have to wait.

As the fall leaves started to show their brilliance, my answering machine did also. It was a message from Cousin Ken. Ken was Pat's oldest and only son. He lived in Michigan, and had gotten word of a surprise cousin, me. He wanted to talk to me. I called Ken, and he indicated, like so much of the family, he had been estranged for a long time and was trying to reconnect to his roots. He grew up in Southern California and went into the service when he was eighteen. As a combat vet, he had been experiencing issues associated with posttraumatic stress disorder and had been working with the Veterans Administration in Michigan since. He was ending a long-term relationship and hoping to get back to California to be with his family. Ken indicated he would be passing through Wisconsin on his way out west, and hoped he could meet me. In the meantime, he agreed to forward a picture of himself at my request.

The next day, when I got to school, I found the email from Ken, with his picture attached. When I opened it, I was amazed. Ken looked a lot like me. It was more than a similarity, Ken looked exactly like me. Maybe it was just his shaved head and a similar facial hair pattern. But even the students I showed it to found it hard to believe it wasn't me. In the picture, Ken and I were nearly twins. It may have explained a lot. When I lived in Southern California, I kept running into people who swore they had seen me before. I never understood it at the time, but seeing Ken's picture shed new insight on the false Fred sightings. Eventually, Ken did stop by on his way to California. Even though we couldn't pass as twins, our looks were similar enough that it was evident we were family.

That Christmas, Sylvia honed in on my supposed Cherokee roots on my paternal side. In addition to a wonderful Cherokee vase that decorated our front hall, she bought a Cherokee book that celebrated the lost civilization of the Cherokees and their heritage. Although it may have only made up a small part of my genetic composition, it seemed to symbolize a lost heritage with a very real past. It seemed to symbolize me.

CHAPTER 10

A SIDE TRIP INTO THE PAST

JUNE 2006

During the spring of 2005, one of Sylvia's students won the state history day competition. It meant she would be moving on to the national competition in Washington, DC, during the summer. The Sheboygan Area School District takes national competitions very seriously and offered to send Sylvia to Washington, DC, to support the student. It seemed they actually felt no child should be left behind. Sylvia talked to me about it, and we saw it as a great opportunity to take a family trip to Washington, DC. I went to DC when I was roughly Grace's age, and I always remembered it as one of the highlights of my early teen years. All the kids would be studying government in middle school, and we thought a trip to the nation's capital might bring a more tangible aspect to their education.

We decided to leave for DC the day after we wrapped up the school year. Before I knew it we were packed up and ready to hit the road. We also decided to take the ferry across Lake Michigan to avoid driving around the lake and through Chicago. Time wise we realized it was a wash, but both of us had spent too much time in unexpected traffic jams, endlessly staring at the distant Chicago skyline. We didn't want to incur that stress so early in the trip; however, our choice brought on an unforeseen kind of stress. The lake was rough, and the tiny ship was tossed.

As we pulled away from the Milwaukee breakwaters, the two-to-three-foot waves were a minor amusement as the kids took turns acting like a pinball, bouncing from side to side as they tried to navigate the isles. But as the Milwaukee skyline disappeared, so, too, did our feelings of amusement while we dreadfully watched the barf bags appear. Neither the kids nor I suffered from motion sickness, but to Sylvia the endless rocking motion was more than she could stomach. I quickly navigated my way to the service counter to scarf up one of the last remaining packs of Dramamine. While the Dramamine effectively eliminated her symptoms of motion sickness, it also eliminated her ability to remain conscious. Sylvia awoke somewhere in the middle of central Pennsylvania, just as the kids finished watching their third movie.

We decided to stop for the night in Breezewood, Pennsylvania, just north of the Maryland border. Located at the intersection of Interstates 70 and 76, Breezewood was the portal to a shortcut to DC, and a popular rest spot for truckers and tourists arriving from the west. Despite its popularity, however, Breezewood seemed to be in the middle of nowhere. Nestled in the midst of the Appalachian Mountains, each protected valley offered little insight as to what lay over the adjoining ridge. Although the mountains on each side seemed to offer protection from the world outside, there also seemed to be a feeling of uncertainty from being unable to see what dangers might be waiting. To me, Breezewood had an eerie feeling. We found a vacant room, grabbed a bite to eat, and marveled at the local color displayed by our server. Something in her demeanor led me to believe she was of a very old spirit. But that seemed to be a common element reflected in Breezewood.

The following morning, I awoke at three. I had long ago gotten use to waking before the rest of the world, and enjoyed the solitude of being the only conscious being. After I consumed the motel room's two microcups of instant coffee, I decided to venture into Breezewood to see if I could find a more substantial stash and get some breakfast treats for the pack. As I stepped out of the protected haven of the motel, a dense misty fog engulfed me. Only the distant orange glows surrounding the street lamps, scattered at various heights displaying a wide array of levels of intensity accompanied me. Yet I felt I was not alone. Someone or something was out there. But I felt more intrigue than fear, as there was a comfort to the presence. As I cased the empty streets, eventually I came upon an all-night gas station manned by its lone attendant. Once I gathered my stash, I returned to the motel to deliver the goods before the peace gave way to calamity. While passing through the motel's vestibule, I glanced at a kiosk housing an assortment of brochures proclaiming the areas various tourist attractions. Although we had a plan for the day, I thought I could pass the remaining moments of solitude gaining insight into the area's attractions. The brochure seemed to open itself to the page that declared the area's most significant and historical attraction. It was Gettysburg. I had been to Gettysburg once before during my return trip from living in DC following my stay with Sean. As I was on a tight timetable, I only gained a passing glance as part of a short rest stop. Something told me I needed to return.

As calamity slowly gained its grip on our room, the power of the powder-sugar coated donuts provided enough of an antidote to propose my plan to Sylvia. She, too, seemed intrigued by the idea, and we altered our day's plan. We would take a slight detour on State Highway 30 to stop in Gettysburg for lunch and a brief tour before proceeding to DC.

We made our way through the rugged Pennsylvania Appalachian terrain and became mesmerized by the narrow, death-defying mountain passes. While the ride was beautiful, it also soon became apparent the dramatic steep inclines followed by peerless free falls, which hugged the sides of the mountains pushed our packed minivan to its limits. We couldn't imagine how entire regiments of foot soldiers could have possibly managed the journey during the sweltering early July days in 1863. It was unfathomable.

We arrived from the north, the same side as the Confederates when they entered Gettysburg. It seemed ironic since I was a Union boy. Did William Jasper Brookshier fight here? I knew he fought in the Civil War, but did he fight at Gettysburg? Did he die at Gettysburg? Was he the presence I felt that seemed to lead me to Gettysburg? When we arrived, we found a burger joint to refuel and put together a plan for our stay. The same local color we experienced in Breezewood seemed to be amplified in our server in Gettysburg. She advised us to start our visit at the visitor center just over Cemetery Ridge. She also told us the electric map was essential. After our burgers we followed her advice and proceeded to the visitor center. We had options.

The open-air tour buses left every hour and completed a two-to-three-hour trek through the battlefields. Our other option was to purchase a self-guided tour book, complete with an instructional CD. Our choice was the latter. While the kids found the concept of the tour bus exciting, Sylvia and I saw it as a potential trap. What would happen if the kids got restless in the middle of the tour? Our self-contained minivan, complete with its DVD system, seemed like the better option. That way we could proceed at our own pace, and the endless drones of "Are we done yet?" and "I'm bored" could be squelched by the movie *Dodgeball*. In the meantime, we purchased our tickets for the electric map presentation and took our seats. The presentation provided an overview of the three-day engagement, which covered the hundreds of acres on which the battles took place. Complete with the dismal statistics of casualties, the presentation provided a framework to begin to understand the enormity of the battle. Sylvia and I were dumbfounded, and the kids became bored. Our decision on the minivan tour option was confirmed.

As we began our guided tour on the northern stretches of the first battlefield, the Confederate side, it began to sink in. We were on a small fragment of the battlefield, yet the land seemed endless. Thousands of men lost their lives here. A high price was paid to gain this little plot of land. We drove over Seminary Ridge, past the northern end of the Peach Orchard and the Wheat Field, and finally began our turn on to the Union's side. The views from on top of Little Round Top were awe inspiring. Sharp, rocky knolls and outcroppings provided natural fortification for whomever would claim the small hill. At the same time, it also commanded the rest of the western battlefields via its strategic position. Devil's Den lay below. It was a hellhole. Finally, as we wrapped our way around the Union position, we came upon the hallowed ground of Pickett's Charge and the Angle. Tens of thousands of men were wounded or died here.

I was haunted by Gettysburg. It got into me. Why had so many given their lives? What did they fight for? It was freedom. It was on the premise that all men were created equal. Ironically, both sides were fighting for freedom. My understanding is the Confederates were fighting for freedom of the autonomy of the states. The Union was fighting for the freedom of the individual and that all are created equal. While the Union clearly won the Civil War, the battles for individual freedoms and rights continue to wage their war today. I still battle that war today.

When we wrapped up our tour, we decided a final stop at the gift shop would complete our visit. Among the maps and trinkets, I spotted a listing of the casualties of Gettysburg. My first search was for William Jasper Brookshier. Did he die here? Is he what led me here? No, he wasn't listed. I proceeded to look for any Brookshiers, Brookshires, Brashears, Owenses, Gentrys, and any other surname I could recollect from my search. I found nothing. While some of the surnames seemed close, I couldn't pinpoint any definitive relative. Whereas I was miffed at my failure, I realized I took away something greater. It was an awareness of what happened here. It was why the Civil War stands so prominent in American history. And it was a greater awareness of my own history.

Fortunately, Gettysburg was only a few hours from Washington, DC. The rest of our trip was spent with Sylvia attending her duties at the national history day competition as I toured the kids around Washington.

During one of the days, Sylvia was able to break at noon, and we decided to tour the National Mall and the Smithsonian Institutions. Among the newer attractions I had not seen before was the Native American Museum. We wound our way through the various indigenous nations and toward the top came upon the Cherokees. I remembered my great-grandfather Owens was reported to be at least a quarter Cherokee via his mother's side. She was from Habersham County, Georgia. It was time for another revelation. This wasn't just American history but it was also my history. The trials and tribulations, the culture, and even the belief structure of the Cherokee Nation were intertwined in my genetic composition and my history. The swift stroke of the pen that rewrote my social history and created my new fake birth certificate didn't touch my genetic history. It was part of me. It was me.

On the way back from DC, we stopped in Toledo to visit John. Once again my nomadic brother had returned home. We stayed in a motel just outside Toledo, which kept the kids occupied with a swimming pool. John came to meet his nieces and nephew, after which John and I headed into Toledo. John had rented a loft apartment in the downtown and took me there for a nightcap at the end of our visit. We talked for a couple of hours, and eventually, it was time for me to head back to the motel. I felt I had gotten to know John a bit better this time. The first time we met, between the awkwardness of the situation and our unfamiliarity with each other, it was difficult to be relaxed and let our guard down. This time the conversations seemed to take a more natural flow and less of an informational exchange. It was the last time I saw John.

As the summer burned on I decided to try a new venture. Maybe it was moving onto an old farmstead, or maybe I had finally connected with my rural roots. The rural lifestyle is one of self-sufficiency and reaping the benefits of the land. We had neighbors who raised their own meat chickens, and it seemed like it was something I could do. Broiler chickens are raised for about eight weeks to maturity, and butchered before they die of other natural causes. Because they have been bread for their rapid growth rate, by the time they reach maturity many start to die due to heart attacks, and others become lame. As I investigated options for raising chickens, I became aware of the movable coop. The chickens were housed in an enclosed movable pen, and moved every two to three days. Not only did the coop protect them from predators but they also continually feasted on a bed of fresh grass. Besides, this way I wouldn't have to shovel chicken shit. It seemed I had already shoveled enough shit in my life.

As I nurtured the hatchlings beyond their incubated pen, I realized it was more than just part of the rural lifestyle that I found rewarding. Many of my neighbors had far more land than I did, and they were very satisfied with their expensive grass-burning ornaments, horses. During my visit with Don's aunt Ina, however, I recalled her telling me Don spent much of his childhood either on his grandfather's farm or his aunt Sally's chicken farm. Perhaps it was another way for me to connect with Don. I actually had come from farming roots on both sides of my family. Not only were both of Don's sides from farming backgrounds but also Maureen's. While she was raised in a city, she had once told me her mother was from one of the oldest farms in the county. I felt my skin was finally starting to fit.

PART IV

PUTTING THE PIECES TOGETHER

CHAPTER 11

LINCOLN, VICKSBURG, AND RON
AUGUST 2006

Ron had resettled just north of Houston and retrieved his belongings, which included Don. Between his urgings and my lessons learned the previous summer, I decided to make the trip to meet him and retrieve Don. Sean and his wife, Robin, also relocated to Houston, so it would provide an opportunity to meet another cousin. As I studied the map in anticipation of my trip, I recognized a straight interstate shot would be the quickest route; however, the trip offered additional opportunities. Since my haunted visit to Gettysburg earlier in the summer, I had become a Civil War junky. I would make two planned stops. The first would be in Springfield, Illinois, and the second in Vicksburg, Mississippi. Springfield was President Lincoln's hometown and contained his tomb. Vicksburg was the last Confederate stronghold on the Mississippi, and to many its fall symbolized the start of the collapse of the South. Perhaps it would also be the beginning of the end to my journey. I was ready for an end. This had gone on too long.

I arrived in Springfield in the late morning. As I navigated my way through the town, I was surprised how buried into Springfield Lincoln's tomb seemed to be. Following the signs and markers, I wound my way through a residential neighborhood to an unassuming gate of an older cemetery. Eventually, I came upon the tomb site. It looked different than I imagined. The tall rectangular structure on top seemed to resemble the Washington Monument, surrounded by a couple of domed buildings resembling the Jefferson Memorial. Besides the caretaker, it seemed there was only one other set of visitors: a mother and her two young boys. The boys seemed more preoccupied with rolling down the grass berm, upon which the tombs structure sat. The mother asked me to take a picture of the three of them, and I gladly accommodated her needs. It had been a long time since my role was that of being requested to take the picture, versus the asker.

Proceeding into the catacombs of the tomb resulted in the feeling of a somber expression, which must have enveloped the country following Lincoln's assassination. Initially, I seemed to notice the familiar smell of a funeral home. Suddenly I felt I was in the presence of greatness. The designers of the monument and tomb did their job well. As I came upon Lincoln's final resting place, an overwhelming notion took hold. His death and the Civil War must not be forgotten. It is every citizen's responsibility to exercise, and fight for the rights Lincoln fought and died for. The same rights and expression of life that so many soldiers had also died for must not be forgotten. The government must exist to serve its people. People's rights must not be forgotten.

Although it was only noon, I felt the crushing impact of the day's work that still remained. Lincoln's Tomb had surpassed my expectations in its impact. I wanted to stay longer, but realized the agenda for my day still required many hours of driving to reach my night's destination, Vicksburg, Mississippi. I planned to arrive in Vicksburg, find a room, and tour the park in the morning. It was to be a very full day.

The rest of the day's drive was fairly uneventful. I crossed the Mississippi at St. Louis, Missouri, and then again in Memphis, Tennessee. In total, my first day incurred about fifteen hours of driving with a two hour stop in Springfield. But to finally meet Ron, and retrieve Don's remains motivated me to push on. As I rounded St. Louis, I started to second guess my plans. The Brookshier farm was just outside Milan, Missouri, which was located in central northern Missouri, just south of the Iowa border. But my fantasy was eradicated by the reality that the side trip would delay my arrival in Houston. Milan would have to wait.

By the time I reached Memphis and the Mississippi border, the sun had made its way to the lower stretches of the western sky. I decided to take what I thought would be a more scenic route on State Highway 1 through rural Mississippi. Several miles north of Memphis I recalled seeing billboards for a Casino in Tunica, located on Highway 1. I also remembered my uncle Rich talking favorably about a trip he and my aunt Betty made to Tunica.

I was not a casino person, although Casinos had been good to me over the course of my life. In the early eighties, I wondered into a gambling parlor while attending a business conference in Las Vegas. As I walked by a craps table, I noticed one of the casino workers was giving a lesson on the game. I watched and realized it was very statistical in nature and decided to give it a try. Over the course of the next several hours, I had gathered about four thousand dollars in winnings. Periodic trips to other casinos over the years following provided similar results. While some would have fallen prey to gambling's addictive powers, for some reason I decided I would remain one of the few people who had beat the odds. I decided I would not stop at Tunica.

The initial deviation on to Highway 1 was scenic, with boulevards of planted palm trees, beautiful rhododendrons and azaleas. But once I passed Tunica, it wasn't long before the tentacles of the casino lost their grip and rural Mississippi showed its true personality. Rural Mississippi is poor. Dilapidated shacks, broken-down cars, and tarped roofs, replaced the palm trees, rhododendrons and azaleas. The farther into the heart of rural Mississippi I drove, the more apparent the poverty became. It became a very depressing ride.

About sixty miles north of Vicksburg, unbeknown to me, I passed one of the last open gas stations. Signs promised another refueling spot twenty miles ahead. I decided my quarter tank of gas could be pressed to make it the extra twenty miles. As the needle on the gas tank and the sun both sunk lower on the horizon, I eventually came upon the promised gas station. But like so many of the other dilapidated structures on my journey, it, too, was boarded up. Perhaps it was another victim of Hurricane Katrina, or just another casualty of a depressed rural southern economy. Either way, I was in trouble. I knew I wouldn't make it to Vicksburg, and I didn't think I could make it back to the last gas station as the low fuel light already displayed a steady glow. I put the truck in park and turned off the engine. I had already taken a two mile detour off the highway and wasn't even sure I would make it back there. It was getting dark, and I was alone in rural Mississippi. C. S. Owens, Don's grandfather, was from rural Mississippi. I started to realize why he may have left. I wanted to leave.

I glanced in the rearview mirror and noticed a black man with a large German Shepherd approaching my truck. I started to grow fearful. "I saw you got Wisconsin plates. You lost?" He inquired with a deep Southern drawl. I explained my plight. He proceeded to explain his sister moved to Wisconsin after the hurricane as a refugee, and she said it was a good place. He also told me the next gas station was about twenty miles down the road, which was why he always carried a spare tank in the back of his truck. He offered to sell me the roughly two gallons left for five bucks, well below the fair market price. I gladly agreed, and gave him the last twenty in my wallet. He offered me change, but I explained the fuel and hospitality he showed me far exceeded the value of the twenty bucks. Within a couple of hours, I arrived into Vicksburg. It had turned dark shortly after my encounter, and I quickly booked a room at one of the motels located just off the highway.

After too many Scotch and waters at the motel's lounge, I stumbled back to my room and crashed for the night. When morning arrived, it did so with a familiar ambiance. The misty fog I remembered from Gettysburg had moved south to Vicksburg. Once again it greeted me as I made my morning pilgrimage to find coffee and something to stifle my stomach's complaints from the previous evening's indulgence in Scotch. As I emerged from the motel's parking lot and headed into Vicksburg, I passed the entrance to the battlefield park. The eerie glow of streetlights shrouded by puffs of fog seemed to beckon my arrival. It would be several hours before the park opened, but I knew it would again be an insightful day.

Eventually, the fog was replaced by a gentle, persistent rain. My first stop was the visitor center. I was the first visitor of the day. While there wasn't an electric map, there was a multimedia presentation that outlined first the attack and then the siege at Vicksburg. Vicksburg was surrounded by a natural fortification of hills, valleys, and berms, which meant its defenders were at a strategic advantage. Once U. S. Grant battled his way to Vicksburg, his only viable option was to surround the city, and cut it off from the rest of the Confederacy. Over the course of six weeks, Vicksburg ran out of food and water. Starvation eventually defeated the Confederates' will, and they surrendered on July 4, 1863, the day after the Army of Northern Virginia had been repelled at Gettysburg. I walked my all too well-known path. *Was this a place where my ancestors lived and died?* But again I found no recognizable names in the death and wounded rolls. During my departing stop at the visitor's center. one of the guides showed me a website I could access to find relatives who fought in the Civil War. I decided it was a task I could complete when I arrived back home. I proceeded to Houston.

Despite the fact I had traveled the bulk of my miles on the first day, the second seemed to take nearly as long to complete. Perhaps it was the anticipation of finally meeting Ron, or maybe it was the remnants of a hangover that made the drive more uncomfortable. Ron had suggested I stop in a small town on the Mississippi named Natchez. I followed his advice and planned it for my lunch stop.

Natchez was a quaint old southern town of the Deep South, with many preserved buildings, which had been spared the burning of the South.

Fortunately, Grant headed toward Atlanta, not Natchez. I found a small pub located below the bluffs overlooking the Mississippi and enjoyed a blackened catfish lunch, along with a pint of Guinness. It seemed to take the edge off the morning. As I enjoyed my southern-style lunch, I overheard the bartender talking on the phone about his endeavors during the previous night. While the content of his conversation seemed to be of a rather crude nature, his particular use of the Southern dialect seemed to give it a gentlemanly flavor. There was an appeal to the South. I began to feel endeared to the southern culture. Perhaps this was what kept so many of my ancestor's south of the Mason-Dixon Line.

Once again I decided on a rural route through Louisiana, and I eventually connected with Highway 10, just east of Lake Charles, Louisiana. Lake Charles was the landfall site of Hurricane Katrina. Even though the hurricane had occurred nearly one year earlier, its devastation was still evident. My route took me on a ferry ride over the Mississippi just south of Natchez. Again the depth of poverty that permeated the Deep South left me awestruck. It also made me realize this was the land that lost. Over one hundred years after the Civil War, the South was still covered with its battle scars. It also struck me that this was the land from which a significant branch of my ancestors came from. Many of my relatives migrated across and were born in the Deep South. Whereas I had been raised a Yankee boy and always basked in the glory of being from the side that won, I now felt a connection to the South. The Civil War left battle scars on more than just the land; many of the souls of the South contained far more devastating scars. Perhaps I was a scar from a descendant of a defeated southern family.

By the time I arrived into Houston, it was already bordering on early evening. I called Ron to announce my arrival and get my final instructions to his home. Ron decided it would be easier to meet at a restaurant near his home where we could grab a bite to eat. He could then lead me the final miles to his home. Besides, he lived in a gated community, and he could register my vehicle if we arrived together. The plan was made. I had seen a couple of pictures of Ron, but I was uncertain I would actually recognize him in person. My shiny chrome dome was easily recognizable, even in a crowded restaurant, so I thought he may have the advantage.

When I arrived at the restaurant, I parked my green Toyota truck in a prominent place so he could be assured I had already arrived. After scouring the parking lot for his powder blue Ford Bronco, I positioned myself at the bar, which allowed me to view anyone entering. After forty-five minutes, I decided to step outside to see if he had arrived. Bingo. Somewhere inside was Ron. I started my way back into the restaurant. Just before reentering I turned back, to see a man open the door of the only powder blue Ford Bronco in the parking lot. It was Ron Bracken.

Ron was a little shorter and thicker than I imagined. As I studied his face, I did see I was starting to understand the "family" look. It was in his eyes. They were similar to mine. They seemed to be similar to what I had come to believe Don's looked like. Ron immediately reiterated Regina's first comment: my eyes were just like Don's. Ron already felt familiar. A few cocktails and dinner later, our conversation seemed to be flowing comfortably. I was enjoying getting to know my uncle Ron. Although Ron grew up in Colorado, he seemed comfortable in the South and didn't think he would ever leave Texas. I recounted my visits to Lincoln's tomb, Vicksburg, and Gettysburg and how after finding out about Don's great-grandfather being in the Civil War I had become a Civil War junky. Ron indicated that he, too, had a great-grandfather who served in the Civil War. It was a great-grandfather we both shared. He was a member of the Texas artillery for the Confederacy. My southern roots had just grown a little deeper.

After the bill was paid, I followed Ron back to his home. Once inside, we were greeted by Sean, Ron's son and my cousin. Sean found my story fascinating and was quite intrigued by the amount of information I had massed about his family—our family. By now the two-day journey had taken its toll, and I was ready for a good night's sleep. Before Ron showed me to my room we stopped in the living room, where next to the couch were two cardboard boxes. Ron explained in addition to the box with Don's ashes and the final elements from the funeral was the box with

Don's stereo, CD collection, and his bowling ball. Ron had told me Don was an avid bowler. Although the thought to open the boxes immediately crossed my mind, exhaustion won, and I decided it would be best to wait for the morning to examine their contents. I knew it would be emotionally dangerous to dive in to Don's life on such little sleep.

The following morning, I awoke before the sun. Perhaps the polite thing to do would be to wait for the rest to awake before I began forging through the boxes. But I didn't think my situation could be found in one of Emily Post's guides to proper etiquette. Like a kid on Christmas morning, impulsiveness quickly took its grip, and I found myself ripping open the first box. A random cross section of Mozart, the Lemon Sisters, and Mario Lanza surprised me. Who was Don Brookshier? He certainly had a wide range in his musical tastes.

As I dug deeper into the box, I spotted a red bowling ball bag with the name "Don" imprinted on a tag hanging from one of the grips. It was Don's bowling bag. Next to it was another bowling ball. I carefully lifted the ball from the box. As I turned over the ball, there between the finger holes was inscribed the name "Fred." Somehow I was transported from the northern outskirts of Houston to the dark side of the moon. Time and space seemed to fold into one. Why did Don have a bowling ball named Fred? That was my name. But, according to Maureen, Don never even knew if I was a boy or a girl. Beyond that, Maureen named me Steven. Maureen didn't even know I had become a Fred. I became overwhelmed by my emotions. I was elated yet furious at the same time. I wished I could have at least met Don. But I couldn't. He had died long before I even was aware I was adopted. Being a rational person, I realized the most likely explanation had nothing to do with me. Yet the coincidence seemed beyond comprehension. Fred was not a common name. I didn't get it.

Minutes later I heard Ron and Sean stirring upstairs. For some unknown reason, I quickly put the contents back in the box and hurried back to the kitchen. I didn't want to be exposed. It wasn't that I planned on not telling Ron I had looked in the boxes, but for some reason I didn't want to be caught in the act. As I made a pot of coffee, Ron emerged with a cheerful, "Good morning." After a short salutary greeting, I blurted out, "I went through the boxes." Ron actually seemed relieved. He was fearful I might not want the stuff and was a bit surprised at my apparent indifference the night before. I explained I actually wanted to examine the contents by myself. Although I already felt quite comfortable with Ron, it seemed like it was something I just needed to do by myself. Ron seemed to understand. Even though Ron had gotten used to expecting the unexpected as far as I was concerned, even he was awestruck by the inscription on the bowling ball. He never really examined it that carefully and hadn't even looked in the boxes since he packed them several years ago, many years before he found out Don had another son. Furthermore, the bowling ball named Fred was as much of a mystery to Ron as it was to me. Sean, the rational lawyer in the crowd, also seemed mystified. He always thought people made up these kinds of things.

I spent the better part of three days with Ron, and periodically Sean would join us. Sean's wife, Robin's, parents were in town, and Sean was doing his best to meet everyone's needs. Ron showed me the taped box with Don's ashes, which had never been opened. After spending some time with me, Ron indicated he felt he made the right decision in giving me the ashes. Although he thought a decorative urn sitting on a fireplace might be a better final resting place, he concurred that Don might like my thought of being buried in the Wisconsin woodlands. Ron reiterated that Don always loved the Wisconsin woods.

The final evening with Ron was spent with many cocktails by his pool, listening to Don's CDs. Ron recounted many tales of times he shared with Don. Although they were many years apart in age, Ron always felt a special connection to Don. He also told me of their mother, and how she would have taken great joy in meeting me. Ron felt it was such a shame she had passed away only months before my discovery. I also told Ron of my youth, and what I had done with my life prior to my discovery. Ron also talked about the Brookshier family. A branch of the Brookshiers, the Brookshires, were a prominent family in Texas and even started a large chain of grocery stores throughout Texas. I was from families to be proud of. Ron welcomed me.

Eventually, it was time to turn in for the night. The hours seemed to pass as though they were minutes. Two, three, and finally four in the morning came and went. I needed to turn in for the remaining few hours of the morning as I had a lot of driving to do later that day. But when Ron went into his room, I decided I would be better off leaving now and grabbing a motel room midday. I figured if I made it up to Arkansas I could cover the remainder of the trip after a few hours of sleep. Besides, I wasn't good at goodbyes, and I could tell this one would be particularly hard. I packed up the truck and was on my way before the sun broke the horizon. Per my nature, I decided to take a rural state highway up through Lufkin to Interstate 30. I could have taken the interstate up to Dallas, but that would have required a somewhat westerly route. I was headed east.

Northeast Texas is comprised of beautiful rolling hills, with many small towns scattered along the highway. As I passed Lufkin and then Longview, I was starting to feel the effects of too many cocktails the night before and no sleep. It was early on a Sunday morning, and most of Texas was still asleep. Somewhere between Longview and Naples, I decided I needed more coffee to fuel my trip to Little Rock. As I pulled into a remote small town, a supermarket ahead seemed to be open. I pulled into the empty parking lot.

A new temptation entered my thoughts. I had to see Don, or at least what was left of him. When I packed up the truck earlier that morning, the only belongings of Don's that made it into the truck cab were Don, a CD by Mario Lanza, and his bowling ball named Fred. When I reached into the back seat and picked up the sealed container holding Don, I thought it was heavier than I would have imagined. I had never held the cremated remains of a person before, so this was a new experience. But at the same time I was taken by the compactness into which an entire life could be squeezed. Yet his life was more than the remaining ashes left from the cremation process. Really, his life was all that he left behind. Not only was it his offspring but also the memories of those who shared in his life. I had become familiar with too many views of those memories through my search. While I was a physical manifestation of the bitter memories of the scorned women he met along his life's journey, I was glad I had pursued meeting the Owens and Brookshier families. Ron had finally filled in the missing pieces. At least now I had a more complete and rounded picture.

As Mario belted out "Beloved" from the play *The Student Prince*, I carefully opened the cardboard box. Inside was another sealed plastic box. My heart was pounding. I broke the seal, and there inside was a plastic bag containing the last remnants of Don Brookshier. I carefully opened the twist tie, opened the bag, and inhaled the first breath the bag had released since it was sealed in 1993. I was with Don. A somber satisfaction enveloped my soul. Even though I hadn't met Don in person, I felt I had gotten to know Don and who he was. I missed him. Before I knew it the CD had progressed to "The Desert Song," and I had been in a trance for the better part of what seemed an eternity. I needed to move on.

After carefully repacking the bag into the box, I proceeded into the market. A fresh pot of coffee was brewing as I searched the aisles for a snack. A cup of coffee and a bag of powdered donuts later, I returned to the checkout. As I proceeded to the truck I felt an eerie presence. It wasn't the same as the presence I felt in the misty fog at Gettysburg and Vicksburg, yet something was there. Something wasn't right and I knew I needed to leave. I put the key in the ignition, gave it a turn, and nothing. Nothing happened. It seemed my battery had suddenly died. I went back into the market, explained my lack of luck, but unlike the cold, wintered North, no one carried jumper cables with them in Texas. I was at least three hours from Ron's house, so I knew I couldn't ask Ron to come and help me. I needed to call a towing service. Fortunately, when Jim completed my last oil change, before I left on my trip, he suggested I purchase his special at the time, which included towing insurance for three thousand miles. I was still within the allotted mileage, so I called Jim. While I waited for the call back from the local service, I went back in the market so I could give the towing service directions to my location. All I knew was that I was somewhere in northeastern Texas at a market. When I received the call and described my problem to the wrecker driver, he took my information, and finally asked, "Where are you?"

I didn't know, so I asked the clerk the name of the market. She replied, "Brookshier Brothers." I was back in *The Twilight Zone*. I wanted to be back in Kansas.

As I completed my journey through northern Texas, I made my final stop for a new battery and a tank of gas at a Walmart Supercenter just outside Texarkana. It seemed I had spent a lifetime in Texas. Arkansas would be a welcome relief; however, my experience in Texas also energized me. I decided to press on. Little Rock came and went. As darkness started to settle in, I crossed the southern Illinois border at Cairo. It felt good to be in the North again. I decided I would spend the night in Carbondale. It had been a very long day.

The next morning, I continued my journey and arrived back home sometime in the late afternoon. It was mid-August, and a new school year would be starting soon. I continued to talk to Ron on a periodic basis. I even called John and Guy to discuss my plans, with which they concurred. Yet I couldn't bring myself to do it. Don had moved from a storage shed in Texas, to the top of a refrigerator in my barn. I occasionally played Don's CDs on the barn's CD player and gave a toast to him. In a way, it was my way of spending time with Don Brookshier. Periodically, I would bring out the bowling ball, and eventually decided it found a new home on my fireplace hearth.

In the meantime, my fascination with the Civil War grew. I spent countless hours browsing the Civil War website I obtained in Vicksburg. First I confirmed William Jasper Brookshier served with the First Missouri Cavalry. Based on the information available, he was stationed in Missouri. He was fighting for the Union; however, it seemed one of his brothers also served in Missouri at the same time. He fought for the Confederacy. Missouri was a split state. I also found my great-great-great-grandfather Charles Joseph Farmer Owens fought for the Confederacy in the Eighth Texas Artillery. It seemed my interest in the Civil War ran deep in my blood.

CHAPTER 12

IT'S TIME TO BURY THE PAST
NOVEMBER 2006

The school year started, and the structure was a welcomed relief. As I
started my fall cleanup, I also decided to clear another trail on the land.
It would be a short cut to what I decided would be Don's final resting
place. He would be buried on a peninsula, at the junction of three ravines,
under the shade of an old oak tree. Ron proposed a second funeral at one
point, but as we talked about it, we both agreed one funeral per life was
sufficient. The trail I had to cut was through a particularly dense patch of
underbrush, which eventually made it through a sumac grove and opened
onto our field at the base of an old row of cedars. As I cut through the
brush, I recalled therapeutic effects of clearing brush had so early in my
journey. Once again I was forging forward to bury a father. Isn't once
enough for this? Why did I put myself through all this? I did it because

I could. I did it because I had to.

Since the time of my discovery, I had witnessed the near death of my daughter, the disintegration and reconciliation of my marriage, and the near-fatal accidents of three friends I had met on the road, along with the death of a former student. Yet I concurrently pressed on with my mission. This mattered. People shouldn't find out they are adopted in their early forties. But I did. People shouldn't be denied the knowledge of who they are. But they are. But my experience was that, as a legitimate issue individual, I had more rights to my factual information about me than I did as an adopted individual. Was I not born equally? Thinking about my experience in Springfield, I didn't recall Lincoln saying, "All men are created equal, unless they are adopted." But those are the views so many of our laws portray. I had gained my information, but at what cost? The process made it clear I did not own my life. My life continued to be owned by the state. In the eyes of society, adults who were adopted were still children.

As the first flurries of winter began to fly, the weather report warned of a deep freeze over the weekend, and that would mean the ground would freeze. It was around midnight Friday, following a night of heavy social engagements. After we returned home, and everyone else found their way to their nighttime havens, I made my way to the barn for a final night cap with Don. Something told me, it was time. Since I retrieved Don, I knew it had to be done, but I enjoyed walking in my barn and giving him a salutary greeting. Even though he never answered back, I felt his presence. I further realized he was in me. Every strand of DNA I carried was that which I shared with Don Brookshier.

A chilling breeze had begun to take hold, and the winds were blowing the last leaves from their branches. We were about to start a new season. I needed to start a new season. I grabbed my shovel and stuffed Don's box under my coat along with a final night cap in my coat pocket. As I proceeded from the field, past the line of cedars, and finally to the peninsula overlooking the three ravines, I sat down and began to uncontrollably sob. I couldn't do it. I had to do it. Would this really end it? I began to second-guess my plans. But this wasn't about me; it was about giving Don a final resting place. After I gathered my composure, I carefully placed Don's box at the base of the old oak tree, and begun to shovel a hole in the rich black soil. He would find peace. At last he would have a final resting place. At last I would find peace. Once the hole was dug, I opened the bag of ashes for the second time since 1993. It was done.

Alone on that peninsula, I sat beneath the old oak tree and peered at the mound of dirt I had worked and toiled for six years to create. Who was Don Brookshier? What was Don Brookshier to me? Obviously, Don was the second half of the biological roots question I had been perusing. But why couldn't I stop after Maureen gave me the name? Why did I ardently rearrange so many priorities in my life to turn every stone? Once I found the name, why couldn't I just let it be? God knows many in my adopted family, and so many others advised me to let it go. But like a child staring at a dangling thread, the temptation was too great. I had to pull the string and watch the pieces of the hidden shroud fall to the ground, and then painstakingly examine each thread to understand every aspect about them. Like a forensics expert, I had to recreate the life of Don Brookshier. I had to get to know Don Brookshier. I had to get to know me.

Growing up adopted and not consciously knowing I was adopted gave me few options. Sure, I was a Nicora. I was proud to be a Nicora. I had been taught to be proud to be a Nicora. But I always knew there was something different. It wasn't better, and sometimes I thought it might be worse, but I was certain it was different. Physically, I somewhat resembled Nic's side when I was young. As I grew older, the adoption gods showed their insight by allowing Nic and I to have the same hairline. It was the convincing icing on the cake. But inside there seemed to be a difference. I had always been more impatient and restless. Once I turned eighteen, I moved from my home in Milwaukee to northern Wisconsin, Illinois, California, Washington, DC, and Minnesota. I had been an industrial engineer, business consultant, architect, and now a teacher. This was significantly different than both Nic and Chic who were born and raised in the same town with few job or career changes. Additionally, I had also been more obsessive than any of my relatives. I had to push far beyond what seemed around me, to be the normal examination of any situation. I could never just leave any stone unturned. Wasn't my reaction to finding out I was adopted a prime example of this? Even my final choice of surroundings highlighted a difference. In the end, I migrated to a rural setting. I enjoyed the solitude of a small town, farming lifestyle. Nic and Chic, and the vast majority of my adoptive family lived in, and enjoyed the hustle and bustle of city life. They enjoyed the density of the urban fabric.

Were these trait differences, or were they the restless angst of a hidden secret trying to emerge? Was it me trying to emerge? I even remembered having dreams about being adopted in my childhood, but always cast them aside and didn't tell anyone. There were many things in childhood I didn't want to talk about because I was embarrassed by them. I was ashamed to be me. There seemed to be different thoughts and notions that I didn't share with anyone around me. Perhaps on some level I was aware I was adopted and was fearful I would be thrown out again if the secret was revealed. Or perhaps it was just a different part of my nature. For some reason I had to keep the secret, as well as myself buried deep inside. Finding out I was adopted finally opened the doors to allow me to explore who I was. I wasn't just searching for Don Brookshier; I was also searching for me.

The Owens family certainly exhibited my impatient, roaming tendencies. Hell, I spent the better part of four years just trying to stay on top of the newest, freshest trail of Ron Bracken. Searching for Edna led me from Oklahoma to Colorado, California, Florida, and back to California. When I finally found Ron, I found out he had nearly as many location changes as his aunt Milly had marriages. Don didn't seem to move around as much, although he certainly made up for it in career changes. From what I could discover, Don had been a paratrooper in the air force, worked construction, managed a bar, been a beautician, and worked as a taxi driver. Another commonality Don and I shared was our love for a tavern. Ironically, Nic always considered pub people to be the bad elements in our society. Don's music tastes also seemed to be as varied as mine. As for Don's father's side, the Brookshiers certainly embodied a rural farming lifestyle. From what Don's father's relatives told me, the Brookshier family farm had been in the family for generations. As far as anyone recalled, the farm Don grew up on was the same farm William Jasper Brookshier worked when he returned from the Civil War. William Jasper Brookshier and so many other ancestors risked their lives to provide a life of freedom and equal rights for their descendants. They deserved to be remembered and recognized for what they gave me. As I reflected on the Civil War, I thought it may have been my driving need for equality to have the same rights as all others that drove me to claim my rightful place in society. Just because I was a bastard didn't mean I was a shameful creature. I realized the concept of a bastard was merely a conceptual constraint created by a prejudicial society. It was the context I needed to understand to gain a deeper understanding of myself, and move on. It was the context I had gained from my search. I now had a deeper understanding of who I was, and where I came from. It had been essential to find and examine my forbidden roots.

I reached in my pocket and pulled out my final nightcap. "Here's to you, Don Brookshier. May you rest in peace."

EPILOGUE

On the morning of March 15, 2022, I received an inquiry regarding my recently submitted genetic DNA sample through Ancestry.com. I had been registered on a different genetic database and had confirmed my biological mother's identity was factual via a genetic connection to her grandson.

However, I had not been able to confirm that my alleged father was indeed my biological father. Given what I had been through because of my late-discovery adoption experience, I had trust issues and needed proof. I thought maybe the Ancestry system might shed some light, and it did. Shelly, a cousin I found in my search on my biological father's side, surfaced as a genetic second cousin. I thought the journey was over. I was wrong.

The email was from Jenneda Love, a name I did not recognize. Her email indicated I had showed up as a genetic first cousin, which meant we were genetically very close. She further explained her father was adopted at birth, and he did not research his biological roots before his early death at the age of fifty in 2008. So she was at a loss to find biological family. As we dialogued via email in the Ancestry system, I discovered her father was born seven months before me in Milwaukee—where I was born. I started to wonder if it was possible that her father and I could be half brothers.

Given that we each came from two parents, I would have to find a shared connection to my biological father's side to verify that was my genetic connection to Jenneda. Jenneda verified Shelly was also listed as a cousin in her database. It was a hit. Her father, Michael, was my older brother. My family grew, again.

Like my biological father and half sister Jane, I was not able to meet him before his death. And while I took some comfort in my newfound awareness, I also felt remorse for loss of the relationship I never got to have. I realized Michael and I not only shared our genetic heritage but also the experience of being adopted. I would have loved to hear his story about his journey and share with him mine.

May you rest in peace, brother.

ACKNOWLEDGMENTS

would like to thank all the family members and friends who lived with
me through the process up through publication. Many kind souls helped
and supported me throughout my journey. I would also like to thank my
parents, Nic and Chic Nicora, who graciously provided a loving home
and a family to grow up in.

ABOUT THE AUTHOR

Fred Nicora has followed a path of unexplained restlessness ignited by undisclosed triggers in his efforts to find the right fit for his own identity and seek truth in his life. Careers explored on his journey include health-care administration, architecture, business consulting, teaching, and his own entrepreneurial endeavors, including starting a fitness-based company and now authoring his story of being thrust into the adoption triangle.

Fred holds a bachelor's degree in business administration, a master's in management technology, a master's in architecture, and a secondary lifetime teaching license via a master's program. Following a traumatic, life-altering event, Fred struggled with addiction to drugs and alcohol, eventually finding sobriety and a need for spiritual, mental, and physical health.

A father of three grown children, Fred currently lives and maintains a small hobby farm in southeastern Wisconsin.